About the Author

Charmian Clift was born in Kiama, New South Wales, on 31 August 1923. She became a journalist on the Melbourne *Argus* newspaper after the war, and in 1947 married novelist and journalist George Johnston.

Early in their marriage they collaborated on three novels: *High Valley* (which won the *Sydney Morning Herald* prize in 1948), *The Big Chariot* and *The Sponge Divers*. Then, in 1954, having lived in London for the previous few years, they took their family to live in the Greek islands. During this period Charmian wrote two accounts of their life there, *Mermaid Singing* and *Peel Me a Lotus*, and two novels, *Honour's Mimic* and *Walk to the Paradise Gardens*.

In 1964 the family returned to Australia and Charmian began writing a weekly newspaper column which quickly gained a wide and devoted readership.

She died in 1969.

Polly Samson is an author, lyricist and a Fellow of the Royal Society of Literature. Her most recent novel, the bestselling *A Theatre for Dreamers*, features Charmian Clift as one of the central characters.

T0312906

Also by Charmian Clift

Mermaid Singing (1956)
Walk to the Paradise Gardens (1960)
Honour's Mimic (1964)
Images in Aspic (1965)
The World of Charmian Clift (1970)
Trouble in Lotus Land (1990)
Being Alone With Oneself (1991)
Charmian Clift Selected Essays (2001)

With George Johnston

High Valley (1949)
The Big Chariot (1953)
The Sea and the Stone (1955,
republished as *The Sponge Divers*, 1956)
The Strong-man from Piraeus (1983)

Peel Me a Lotus

Charmian Clift

Introduction by Polly Samson

MUSWELL
PRESS

Peel Me a Lotus first published in 1959 by Hutchinson

This edition published by Muswell Press in 2021

Copyright © Charmian Clift 1959
Introduction © Copyright Polly Samson 2021
Illustrations by Nancy Dignan

A CIP catalogue record for this book
is available from the British Library.

ISBN 9781838110123
eISBN 9781838110147

Additional typesetting by M Rules
Printed and bound by CPI (UK) Ltd, Croydon CR0 4YY

The right of Charmian Clift to be identified as the
author of this work has been asserted in accordance with
the Copyright Amendment (Moral Rights) Act 2000.

5 7 9 10 8 6

For
George

Peel Me a Lotus by Charmian Clift

Charmian Clift arrived on Hydra in late August 1955 with her husband George Johnston and their children and decided to stay and live on whatever could be made from writing. Hydra, in those days, was a four-hour steamer ride to the mainland, a mainly barren rock shaped 'rather like a set of well-curved mustachios and cruelly fanged with sharp mountains'.

The island is ten miles long and, despite its name, almost waterless. They were only the second foreigners to buy a house there. Very little English was spoken and Johnston and Clift possessed only rudimentary Greek. It was audacious as well as romantic, especially with a young family, to attempt a free and creative life in the sun.

This book, her second (if we discount the three earlier novels written in collaboration with George Johnston), brings us to an island on the brink of change in 1956. Clift and Johnston were at the vanguard of what was soon to become a fabled bohemian community of artists and writers, of exiles and dreamers.

She was thirty-two years old, her first book, *Mermaid Singing*, a memoir of the family's first year in Greece, on the island of Kalymnos, had been published to some excellent reviews. She was unexpectedly pregnant again. Her husband, in her opinion at least, was giving Hemingway a run for his money, but still the sales of his books – and hers – were poor. The children, though beautiful and free, weighed on her heart 'like lead, like chains, like three strong anchors bedded deep in the reality from which I can never escape.' Clift thought of herself as an Icarus, a yea-sayer, who flew close to the sun but she later referred to this period when she should have 'taken wings and started to fly' as a year when she found herself, once again, 'bound and constrained' by her domestic rites.

The original dream, that the island be a base from which they'd set sail and explore, was starting to fade. She didn't expect to find herself marooned on a rock without so much as the ferry fare to Athens.

'Thank God the delights of anticipation never pall on us: some of the very pleasantest hours I can ever remember have been spent crouching over the charcoal tin, planning courtyards, sailing-boats, making summer trips to islands yet unseen ...' Sometimes it seems that she's writing herself back into a place where hope and good humour flourish but often, especially while waiting for her baby to be born, the lack of a safety-net is palpably vertiginous.

As with *Mermaid Singing* she is writing events almost as they are happening to her. It's a warm and intimate voice that invites us to huddle beside her over the glowing charcoals while Athena's little owl drops liquid notes from the mountains and the huge shapes of cats slinking in the alley are like 'an emanation of the secret soul of the place.'

In describing her wintering companions, she treads an enjoy-ably spiky line between mockery and affection. Henry Trevena is the Australian painter Sidney Nolan. Her portrayal of Ursula, based on his wife Cynthia, was friendship ending: 'grown some-what Gothic and malevolent lately ... and no damn wonder, because he would pour pitch over her and set her alight if he needed a torch to paint by!'. Sean Donovan is writer Patrick Greer and Lola is Nancy Dignan whose drawings head the chapters of this book. 'Jacques' is the painter Jean Claude Maurice 'a little curly dog on heat' who would later be exposed by George Johnston as Clift's lover, (and the source of his own debilitating sexual jealousy), in two of his novels.

Film-makers have started to zero in on Hydra, the quality of the light, its unspoilt beauty and cubist white houses that are arranged in tiers from the port, giving the appearance of a perfect amphitheatre. Clift can sense what is happening to the island as more and more people arrive. She saves her most biting scorn for the film crew (the film that's being made in the later chapters of this book is *Boy on a Dolphin* and the star is an eighteen-year-old Sophia Loren) and for the drifting existentialists who have 'all met Rilke's wife' or Dali, have 'questing, amoral eyes' and a ready fund of scandalously funny stories. 'The war generation who grew up to horror and inherited despair and disillusion.'

By contrast, many of those young newcomers to the island remembered Clift and Johnston as the most helpful of welcoming committees. When a twenty-five year-old Leonard Cohen arrived on Hydra in April 1960 he initially stayed in their spare room and later described how the local people had a great respect for the couple, 'because they lived as the islanders did' and that new people 'stopped at their table in Katsikas' bar to drink with them and get advice – on everything from where to buy their kerosene to what chemical to use to stop the toilet smelling. They were the focal point for foreigners on the island. They had a larger than life, a mythical quality. They drank more than other people, they wrote more, they got sick more, they got well more, they cursed more and they blessed more, and they helped a great deal more. They were an inspiration. They had guts. They were real, tough, honest. They were the kind of people you meet less and less.'

Clift is a sensuous writer, ecstatic at times. When she is gloomy the sea offers salvation; there is always the promise of immersion and renewal. 'Morning and evening the harbour front seems to slip and slide in a moving green-gold mesh of water reflections.' Diving from the high rocks offers a moment of freedom. Night-swims 'where the briny stars wake at a movement' work like balm. In 'the daily never-failing magic of the gulf' her thoughts become most powerfully poetic. She finds herself yearning for oblivion as she swims in a storm 'filled with something that is terror and desire both ... to ride on with the wild wild horses to the waiting cliff, or to curl up small, close against the scaly rocks, to curl up small and let the wild horses ride over me.'

Peel Me a Lotus is strikingly different in tone from *Mermaid Singing*; her darkest thoughts are never far from the surface. When the mad moon 'begins to shine on us with her other face' the original dream of escape darkens to a Boschian vision where angelic little girls called Aphrodite and Persephone crouch together dropping stones on new-born kittens, where eyes are white with trachoma, a baby dead of malnutrition is a swollen toad, where there should be a hand there's a grotesque claw, and 'all the bright young people who throng the café tables suddenly have the ultimate obscenity of necrophilia'.

Clift's original title for this book was 'A Handful of Quietness' from Ecclesiastes, which begins:

'Again, I observed all the oppression that takes place under the sun. I saw the tears of the oppressed, with no one to comfort them. The oppressors have great power, and their victims are helpless. So I concluded that the dead are better off than the living.'

It goes on to envy the unborn, and ends with this advice: 'Better to have one handful with quietness than two handfuls with labour and a striving after wind.'

Handfuls with quietness were hard to come by in Clift's world, labouring as she was on the rocky road between first and second wave feminism, with no steady income and frustratingly torn between her many roles. She reports that she feels an enjoyable melancholia in imagining her own funeral cortege toiling up the mountain path among the rocks and the olives, the chanting priests, the bells and herself 'stretched out among the flowers, stiff and white as a freshly pulled garlic stalk.' She goes further into the future that doesn't contain her. George is to marry again, 'a Greek girl with a satisfactory dowry', she even claims to have a prospect in mind.

This is a book that is inescapably haunted by what is known of its author's death. It's unfortunate that, as she rather prophetically wrote in a later essay, 'A whole human life of struggle, bravery, defeat, triumph, hope, despair, might be remembered, finally, for one drunken escapade.' Suicide throws a long shadow and it's Clift's deepest thoughts about existence that inexorably darken and bloom here like wine through water.

Polly Samson 2021

Peel Me a Lotus

February

I

Today we bought the house by the well.

This purchase, which has been hanging fire for anxious weeks while we have been trying to organise our impossible finances, was finally completed in the office of the notary public, who is also the magistrate of this small Greek island, the municipal valuer, and the husband of my son Martin's favourite teacher at the village school called the Down School to distinguish it from the Up School on the mountain ridge.

The notary public is a small, courteous, asthmatic man. Like all the other town officials he conducts his business in one of the cells of the old monastery that lies behind the gay façade of waterfront shops, and here in the monastery cell we gathered formally as the great bronze bell was crashing noon over our heads.

Behind the desk the notary public, very affable and important, and ranged in a row before him on five spidery black chairs of the old island pattern the five interested parties to this affair: Socrates the carpenter and occasional real-estate agent; Demosthenes the shifty-eyed barber, acting on behalf of the former owner of the house; old Creon Stavris, there to guide us through the final intricacies of the purchase; and my husband George and I, both smoking rather nervously and conscious that we looked a ragged and scruffy pair.

The notary public, old Creon, Demosthenes the barber, and even Socrates, had apparently put on their best clothes for the occasion, and the barber twirled between his fat fingers a crisp white spike of hyacinth.

Still, scruffy or not, we were the purchasers, and it was with some ceremony that we were bowed to the table to sign and swear a large number of incomprehensible documents in Greek, which the notary public read through at a furious wheezing pace and Creon approved by a series of curt nods directed at George. Through the door of the office I could see the heavenly cerulean blue of the balcony ceiling, three thin marble columns, and a tree of hibiscus blazing away in the courtyard beside the ornate tomb of one of the island's innumerable naval heroes.

It seemed a fine thing to be buying a house here.

The price of the house was one hundred and twenty gold pounds, as had been agreed earlier during lengthy and mysterious negotiations between Socrates and the barber. Rather to my surprise there was no last-minute attempt by either of them to raise it ten pounds or so. Perhaps experience is deceitful after all, and one has become unnecessarily devious in business dealings with the Greeks. All the same, it would have been too much to expect that we should catch fortune's tide at the full: the rate of exchange on the gold pound was higher this morning than it has been for months, so that the house actually cost four hundred and ninety-three pounds ten shillings in English paper money, or six hundred and twenty Australian pounds, or about thirteen hundred dollars.

We had to work it out in a variety of currencies because our income derives from slender royalty cheques in several countries, and it was necessary to be quite sure we could really afford to buy a house. In fact, it seemed fairly clear that the purchase was lunacy in any currency, but one hundred and twenty pounds doesn't *sound* much when you say it fast and leave out the rich chink of that word 'gold'.

It was only when I saw it translated into high stiff stacks of new *drachma* notes, which George fished out in handfuls from an old battered briefcase of kangaroo hide that I had given him one birthday long ago in Australia, that my heart lurched slightly.

There it went! Our last little bit of capital, our going-back-to-civilisation money, our reserve against children's illnesses, tonsils or appendix operations, dental disasters — or that never-mentioned contingency that might arise if all does not go well at the birth of this new baby of mine within the next few weeks and I have to be carted off dramatically to Athens in a caique.

The doctor I saw last month in Athens said I could have the child on top of Mount Olympus with absolute safety, and I know that the younger of the island's two midwives is a practical and level-headed woman, and that most of the world's population enters it without the aid of anaesthetics or asepsis, and it is, after all, my third child. But still ...

I must say George flung down the money with quite an air, just as if it was truly one hundred and twenty glittering golden sovereigns he was scattering across the notary public's table. I think at that moment his courage, which has been flagging a bit during the last weeks of these negotiations, was warmed by the fine brave glow of his own audacity. When one has had a lifetime's conditioning in terms of building societies, insurance policies, and second mortgages, it *does* seem to be a reckless romantic thing that the first piece of earth one has ever owned in all the world should be Greek earth, and that one should pay for it — figuratively, anyway — in golden sovereigns, at a time when the Cyprus issue is becoming more venomous every day and they are making bonfires of Union Jacks in Athens and everything English is hated with an intensity that is in directly inverse ratio to the love the English used to command in Greece: everything, that is, except the golden sovereign. The people of this island are inclined to be suspicious — rather narrow-eyed, watchful people they are — and there is no other money they really trust.

There is no bank in the port, so when they acquire the coveted pieces of gold they must hide them away in socks or beneath loose floorboards. There was even some talk earlier that the owner of the house was going to insist on being paid in gold, and Creon was quite prepared to take us from house to house buying up the requisite number of sovereigns. It turned out not to be necessary, for which I was truly sorry.

And after all, I thought, sitting very upright in the chair so that my old duffel-coat hung straight from my shoulders and

8

disguised slightly the sudden alarming activity that was going on under it, one hundred and twenty pounds — even *gold* pounds — wasn't really so much to pay for nine sunny rooms (eight when we have knocked down the wall between the two top-floor rooms and made one big studio) and a long flagged kitchen with an arched stove and a beamed ceiling. In England or Australia now a hundred and twenty pounds would scarcely buy an outhouse. There is a terrace on the third floor, too, that looks clear across the blue gulf to the mountains of Troezen. And the house has a little walled garden with two grapevines and eight fruit trees. The two big children will share a nursery the size of a ballroom, and on the second floor, opening off the room that will be our bedroom, there is a small, sunny space, reached conveniently by a ladder and trap-door from the kitchen, that will make a night-nursery for this unborn one whose present agitation makes me slightly apprehensive. I would rather it waited the few weeks that must elapse before we can move into the new house. There has been too much already of rented houses. I would like at least one of my children to be born in its own home ...

After Demosthenes the barber had suspiciously counted every note in every stack and stowed it away sheaf by sheaf into a cardboard suitcase, and the notary public had locked away *his* pile of bills representing legal fees and tax in an official-looking black box, and Socrates, chirruping with embarrassment, had blushingly slipped his commission money into his pants pocket and Creon had received the formal one *drachma* for acting as witness, the notary public brought down the official seal with a great thump on to a drippy little spread of red wax, and handed us the splendid documents.

Old Creon, who had sat stiff and frowning and official throughout the proceedings, bull neck thrust forward belligerently, now folded his spectacles with slow deliberation, placed them in their neat, embroidered case, and then leapt suddenly to his feet and flung his arms wide.

'*Kalo riziko!*' he cried, embracing us each in turn.

'*Kalo riziko!*' wheezed the notary public, pumping our hands.

'*Kalo riziko!*' giggled Socrates, quite overcome that he had at last actually brought off this deal — or any deal! As a house-agent Socrates is not notably efficient. But then he is even less efficient as a carpenter, and since he hates carpentry and loves houses, old Creon and other citizens of standing like to encourage him in his Chaplinesque real estate business.

Socrates, small, plump, bald, and beaming, in some ways belongs to the whole town, as the whole town belongs to Socrates. He came here as a child, an orphan refugee from the Turkish massacres in Asia Minor, and was adopted by a childless widow, a formidable woman known as Aunt Electra. Aunt Electra apprenticed Socrates to the trade of carpentry, but even as a boy he liked best to go down to the port to watch the boats coming in, to carry bags for passengers, to show strangers where they might obtain rooms.

His pride in the town of his adoption was overwhelming. As he grew older he made it his business to look after the port flags and the decorative strings of bunting that are draped from churches and shopfronts on feast days.

And it is still Socrates who decks the town for great and small occasions, and still Socrates who meets the boats, and still Socrates who skitters along the waterfront and up and down the steep steps and narrow lanes of the town from morning until night, with anxious tourists panting at his heels. His enthusiasm for the island has never lessened. He mourns the vanished glories that he never knew, disguises shabby corners with more and yet more flags, and tries to sell decaying houses to foreigners who might restore them.

These deals, more often than not, are ruined by his over eagerness to display the beauties of the property and his tendency to tell immense and giggling lies about the contents and capacity of water cisterns, the condition of roofs and piping, and the state of sanitary arrangements. Occasionally a deal comes off in spite of him. So today Socrates giggled more uncontrollably than ever while pocketing his commission, and blushed too, for he will work just as hard to sell a house without any commission at all.

'*Kalo riziko! Kalo riziko!*'

And the barber, sidling out of the monastery cell with the cardboard case tucked under his arm, turned at the door and murmured suavely over his shoulder, *'Kalo riziko!'*

'And now,' said Creon, advancing one pointed polished shoe as though he might begin a waltz, 'I take it that we will adjourn to Katsikas' Bar? If everyone is agreed that this is the proper procedure on this most happy and propitious occasion?'

Creon learned his English at Robert College in Constantinople early in the century, and until we came to the island last year he hadn't used a word of it since 1911, so that everything he says has a sort of jaunty formality, very Edwardian and hansom-cabbish, like his clipped moustache and his neat grizzled coiffure and his shabby but beautifully brushed overcoat with its velvet collar and the little sprig of hyacinth in the lapel. But his bulging, short-sighted eyes are shrewd, the forward thrust of his rather flat head on its thick, short neck contentious, and he walks aggressively, cleaving the mild island air with hunched shoulders as though he is forcing a path through some formidable opposition invisible to everyone else.

So he led us out of the notary's office, making a path for us into the light, daring the world to prove if it could that we were not absolutely, legally, indisputably, and if necessary over his dead body defending our rights, sole owners and possessors of the house by the well.

'Kalo riziko!' George whispered to me as we trooped after Creon down the stairs and into the glittering white well of the monastery courtyard and the cold dazzle of early spring sunshine and the red splashes of hibiscus burning away against a cool procession of columns white under the blue balconies. 'Welcome home at last.'

2

Katsikas' Bar is six deal tables at the back of Antony and Nick Katsikas' grocery store at the end of the cobbled waterfront by the Poseidon Hotel, and it is here that we usually gather at midday among the flour sacks and oil jars and painted tin water tanks and strings of onions and soft white festoons of cotton waste: a sort of social club evolved from the necessity to relieve the boredom of an island winter.

The club has a variable membership which fluctuates around the solid nucleus of Creon, his wife Zoë, and the four foreigners, apart from George and me, who have seen out the whole winter here.

If there is a president I suppose it is Creon, who comes to this social half hour of the day now, after four months, as spry and jaunty as if we had all just met, and just as eager to tell again the gay-dog stories of his youth. Curious stories they are, with a strange faint perfume of pomade about them, peopled with mysterious unreal characters who own carriages and steam yachts and French mistresses and spend their spare time buying politicians and gold pounds and magnums of champagne. Through endless repetition Creon's stories have come to have the haunting familiarity of the fairy tales one heard in the firelight so many lives ago.

Creon himself has a history with that same illusive fairy-tale charm of unreality. Born to great wealth, and inheriting in his youth a sponge empire that stretched across Europe and the Americas, he was the last of the island's merchant princes: the final healthy stalk seeded from the dazzling golden crop of great names and greater fortunes that sprouted inexplicably from this singular small grey rock in the brilliant commercial summers of the eighteenth and nineteenth centuries and was withered away by the twentieth. Even when Creon was a child some of the great houses must have been caving in.

Still, he had his brilliant summer too. He built another storey on to the austere stone house his father had left him, added curly balconies and grand stairways, travelled in far countries, bought diamonds in Amsterdam, frail glass in Russia, tweed knickerbockers in England, furniture in France, experience in America. He had the old carved ceilings of the house plastered over and painted with bright pink garlands, and because he despised slightly the fine dark spidery furniture the earlier island aristocrats had plundered from eighteenth-century Europe he

12

went in for plush sofas, love-seats of ruched blue satin, velvet curtains with bobble fringes, ponderous mahogany buffets, porch suites of curly cane, smoking-den chairs, wicker whatnots. Then, having found a suitably bred and healthy young woman among the choice blooms of Athenian aristocracy, he installed her among the Edwardian horrors he had perpetrated in that lovely old house, and went off to New York to attend to his sponge business.

When he returned to his native island some years later with the conviction that his wife had taken recourse to the only diversion possible to a bored and pretty young matron he made no scenes, but supervised her packing himself and escorted her personally to the jetty where his liveried boat crew was waiting to row her to the private yacht that removed her from the island, and Creon's sight, for ever.

He paid back the sum of her dowry into an Athens bank and spent the next twenty-five years fighting her through every court in Europe and America because he refused to pay her an allowance besides. As judgment after judgment went against him he deliberately and implacably broke up his business and ruined himself, rather than let his wife have the satisfaction of wealth and position to which he had decided she had renounced all claim by her behaviour.

The Second World War and the Occupation finished off what was left of his fortune. At the end of it he was a poor man. And ironically enough his wife was dead — old and triumphantly virtuous to the last. When Creon was free to marry Zoë, the gentle little curator and librarian of the island museum, who for eighteen years had submitted equably to a curious series of tests and traps devised to test her virtue and devotion, he had nothing to offer her but his stubborn old age and the great gloomy decaying mansion of his glorious days.

In this house, usually referred to as The House of Usher, Creon and Zoë live still, alone and without servants. The ruched satin love-seats are faded now to dust colour and split along every intricate fold, but Zoë sings as she sits among the tarnished splendours, calmly darning Creon's socks under the single naked light-bulb that hangs pendant from stained and mildewed pink garlands.

She is a broad-faced, simple kind woman of early middle age, whom Creon sees through some mysterious alchemy of love as a kind of eternal Hermia — little and fierce. He is very arch and gallant with her. Finding happiness so late in life he loves with a touching parody of his youth's spryness, desperately willing a gulf in time. I must say Zoë bears it very well: she is largely tolerant of everything, even love's absurdities. So Creon sings too, nostalgic snatches from *The Belle of New York*, as he potters about in the vaulted kitchen warming milk for Zoë on the trumpery little kerosene burner set solitary in the huge arched stove recess where once whole sheep were roasted on the spit, or sits alone at the great dusty desk in the study, surrounded by queer paperweights, strange stiff, dry sponges, ornate inkstands that hold nothing but crusted powders of violet, green, and red. From the top of the bookcases a stuffed albatross, tethered by its spread, half-bald pinions in a thick grey veil of cobwebs, looks down on him with mad glass eyes.

There is no longer any business of his own to transact in the study, but Creon cannot quite stop being a businessman. Gradually, and with increasing authority, he has taken over all the business difficulties of the island's foreign residents — permits, passports, papers, currency entanglements, house-hunting, all legal matters. Not one of us would dare to initiate a business transaction, or even order the winter wood supply, without first consulting Creon. His step is never firmer, his eye never more piercing, than when sorting out our alien problems. It has given him a new appetite for life. He has come to seize upon newly arrived foreigners almost with the avidity of Socrates. Socrates wants to sell them houses. Creon wants to manage their lives.

3

Of the four other foreigners living here, two have been friends of ours for many years. These two, a painter named Henry

Trevena and his wife Ursula, came here last November largely on our recommendation of the island as a place of great beauty which was cheap enough and quiet enough for Henry to put in an undistracted winter's work. Yet in spite of Henry's immediate passion for the high, harsh beauty of the mountains soaring up from the jewelled crescent of the port — truly Greek mountains these, stark and noble, with the violets and golds seeping over them at sunset, and little white droppings of monasteries perched dizzily high on their scarred and pitted slopes — and in spite of Ursula's constantly reiterated intention of refusing to budge ever again, these two are only temporary islanders.

There will be no rest for them anywhere in the world while Henry's impossible vision burns before him, and he pursues it, devouring space and time, beating his own stubborn trails, creating out of his urgency pillars of smoke and fire to guide his ruthless way. Still boyish of face, charming and friendly of manner, with the winningness of the Celt, the dreams, the poetry, and that particular diffidence of the self-educated man groping for articulateness, he is, nevertheless, as implacable as God. If Ursula, has grown somewhat Gothic and malevolent lately, one feels that it is excusable on grounds other than the common one of island boredom. She is worn out, poor Ursula, and no damn' wonder. Henry would pour pitch over her and set *her* alight too, if he needed a torch to paint by!

The other two of the wintering colony are Sean Donovan, an Irish schoolmaster, and his artist wife Lola: washed up on this Greek island by God knows what freakish current and marooned here through lack of funds to move on elsewhere — or by Sean's disinclination to go back to schoolteaching until he has tried to live as a freelance writer.

Something of the key to Sean lies in this. Lola, who is a gusty, opulent, garrulous woman, warm-hearted and dogmatic, is motivated always, one feels, by her inclinations. Sean is motivated by disinclinations. Lola has tastes, clearly stated. Sean has distastes. Sean is not pale: he has charm, sweetness, a perfect intellectual honesty, and a wry Irish humour that is often directed wickedly at Lola. Yet there is something discouraged in him, something of the victim — of his own uncompromising standards, his own lucid reasoning, and, inevitably, of Lola's exasperated nagging.

Every one of us, in his particular way, is a protestant against the rat race of modern commercialism, against the faster and faster scuttling through an endless succession of sterile days that begin without hope and end without joy. Each of us has somehow managed to stumble off the treadmill, determined to do his own work in his own way. Sitting among the bean sacks in an island grocery store, we have become very fond of one another, in the manner of people who by their very presence bolster up the other's sometime flickering conviction.

There are others too who intermittently join the midday group in Katsikas' Bar. There are always several of the lazy, ragged, odd-job islanders; the neat and deferential Civil Servants; strange, brown-faced shepherds down from the mountains; impoverished aristocrats of famous lineage who still maintain their great houses here, even if only as weekend retreat's from the Athens flats where the new world of commerce has cornered them. Then there is old Vassilis, a crippled sponge diver who did brave things with limpet mines in the war and, as a result, carries scars from Buchenwald. There is the director of the School of Fine Arts, who makes periodic winter visits if there are any artists staying at the school; and the artists themselves, winter strays who usually spend a few days here before drifting on to the other Schools of Fine Art which the Greek Government has established at Mykonos and Rhodes and Delphi, or succumb entirely to the curious lure of this island and move out from the school into one of the lovely little whitewashed houses around the port which can still be rented for a pittance.

Just now the school is practically empty — summer is the time when the artists will really invade the port — sheltering under its lofty, carved ceilings only three huge, earnest Swedes, all very young and pink under the pale fuzz of growing golden beards and deadly keen on culture, and a finical French pansy who has found his way here improbably from a small primitive village in the Peloponnese. We are all getting to like Hippolyte in spite of his pink toenails and tight jeans and classic Roman haircut. Under his affectations and social snobberies he is as moral as a French spinster, and his manners shame all of us, who have grown something careless with island living.

Today the group was confined to our own four intimate friends, all drinking wine at the scratched green table in the corner by the kerosene drums, all of us surrounded by our market baskets, oil flasks, and wicker jars filled either with wine from Attica or with kerosene for the cheap little explosive stoves we cook on. The two dogs sprawled under the table — Alexander the Great, a spivvy little half-Pomeranian runt who belongs to the Donovans by right of inheritance, and our own Max: something pointer and something unidentifiable, a goofy, sad-eyed creature, still desolate at being locked out from the notary's office.

Beyond the table, seen surrealistically through bundles of garden rakes and an organ-pipe arrangement of ecclesiastical wax candles, there was a donkey-train jingling along, two crimson caiques unloading vegetables onto straw mats spread along the quay, a coloured kite tugging the sky above the old cannons on the headland. On the other side of the smooth spread of water that lies between our island and the mainland, a thick crust of snow swept down through the dark pine forests to the sea.

'By God, it's a day!' said George smugly, owning it.

'Sit down and stop being landed gentry. You haven't bought the day too.' Lola was plaiting a chain of flowers across her vast bosom, like an exuberant and outsize Flora come incongruously to rest among the shovels and flour sacks. She and Ursula had been scrambling among the ruins on the high slopes all the morning, and the table was heaped with the wildflowers they had gathered from among the stones: curious little striped green orchids like cobras' heads, blood-red anemones, narcissus, pink hyacinth, strange, delicate striped trumpets and spikes, brown bells on acid yellow stalks almost as fine as hair, daisies yellow and white, minute pale violets.

Ursula, hunched in withdrawn and angular concentration over a stack of letters and bills just collected from the post office, had a single almond petal caught in the severely dragged mass of her fine black hair. It fluttered tremulously above her high, lined brow like a scrap of torn pink silk.

Nick Katsikas' plump young wife Polyxena leaned over the back of Ursula's chair, mopping rags suspended, trying to read across her shoulder. Henry was interestedly doodling an abstract pattern in jet-black squid ink on the plate they had been eating from. Sean smiled his sad clown's smile at us as he passed a slip of paper over Ursula's head to Polyxena.

'Thank you, Kyrios,' said Polyxena warmly, examining the paper with baffled interest. 'But what is it? I cannot read it.'

'It is an interesting little paper that goes by the name of a rejection slip, Polly dear,' Sean said. 'If you like it I can give you many more. This one has a particular virtue in being quite fresh, but they're all the same really. They have no practical value whatever, being much too cheaply printed on nasty paper to use even in the privy. But there is a moral lesson to be derived from them. I'm probably aggrieved because it's another printed one,' he added, turning to George. 'I thought this time I might fly as high as a personal note, written with a real pen and ink.'

'Your novel?'

'Oh the hell with it,' Sean said. 'What about the house?'

'Try this one, Polly. It's in Greek.' George handed her the house deeds. Unabashed, Polly wiped her hands on her apron and opened the document.

'Nicko! Nicko! They've bought the house! *Kalo riziko*, Kyrios Giorgios. *Kalo riziko*, Kyria. And to the dear children. Nicko, bring some wine! Dionyssos, read what it says here! Hey, you, Lefteri, come here and read this!'

The house deeds were passed from table to table, and handed on the length of the store to the customers at the grocery counter.

'One hundred and twenty pounds! *Panaygia mou!*' Dionyssos, the garbageman, whistled softly. 'You must be rich all right, Kyrios Giorgios!'

'Po-po-po-po! *Rich!*' Lefteri the house-painter made exclamatory circles with his hand. 'Isn't Kyrios Giorgios rich all right, Kyrios Creon? Isn't he?'

Creon frowned judicially, neither affirming nor denying. Socrates giggled. Of course George was rich. All foreigners are rich. It is an initial Greek concept.

Polyxena hoisted her bulk around the table, so she could lean forward and prod my belly.

'Soon, eh, Kyria? Good freedom to you. And a good beginning in your new house.'

'Good freedom!' everyone chorused. 'And a good arrival in your house!'

'A good arrival,' Lola said, slipping the chain of flowers over my head and twisting the garland with little fat capable hands.

'A good arrival,' said Henry, looking at us in that sudden blue curious way of his, as if we were new and strange after all, and might be worth re-examination.

'A good arrival,' said Sean, bobbing the wild shock of his greying hair in a queer little salutation.

'Oh God, Henry!' said Ursula. 'We *must* find a house too. We must! I won't be dragged about the world after you any more. Creon, you *must* find a house for Henry and me!' Ursula is inclined to play the great lady with Creon, as if she had mentally pigeonholed him among gallery managers, publicity agents, and the potential buyers of Henry's lesser works. She sometimes taps his hand with her spectacles, and even reads him choice or chatty bits from the dozens of letters she receives daily. For months she has been bedevilling him about houses. Now in her sudden cry was a new note of urgency, compelling in its absolute sincerity.

But Creon, feeling perhaps that something more was needed to mark the occasion, had already risen to his feet like a dapper toastmaster and with his glass raised high was full swing into the chorus of 'For They Are Jolly Good Fellows', so he didn't hear her. The others joined in raggedly, as embarrassed as ever that silly song makes people. The locals applauded with great warmth.

They seem to be genuinely pleased that we have bought a house on their island. Perhaps this matter of the house, and the fact that our children go to school with theirs, makes us closer to them, more understandable. For all they see of family life among foreigners who pass this way they might well believe that all Europeans propagate their species in the manner of the single-celled amoeba, by spontaneous division.

Just then the lane door of the shop burst open, and my two children flew in, still in their buttoned school smocks and carrying their satchels, and wild to know if we had truly truly bought the house. So they must have lemonade to drink to the house too and we must all go this minute, this very minute, to open the house and walk around in it and choose what rooms we will have for our own.

'And for B,' Shane murmured lovingly, patting my duffel coat. 'And a nice little room for B.'

Ursula, gathering together her sheaf of letters and the strewn wildflowers, said suddenly: 'Oh yes, you might as well give him a nice little room. He's committed too.'

And for the second time my heart gave that sickening little lurch. For in spending all our capital we had indeed burnt the last boat. Had one really intended to commit oneself so irrevocably? After eighteen months of brave chittering on the subject of the fine free independent life, I stood at the back of Nick Katsikas' grocery store with my belly very great with a new responsibility and my mouth gone dry with surprise and terror.

George, with one child tugging at his hand and the other at his trouser leg, was buying beakers of wine for everyone in the shop. He looked flushed, excited, happy. There he was, and there was I, and there were the children, two and eight-ninths of them, Jolly Good Fellows all. Committed.

4

This is the island to which we are committed. There are many among the thousands of islands of Greece, now arid and virtually waterless, of which ancient poets wrote in terms of sylvan glades, running streams, and nymph-haunted forests. This island could never have been such a one. I feel that it has always been as it is now, a long, bare rock shaped rather like a set of well-curved moustachios and cruelly fanged with sharp mountains: an island completely lacking in fertile soil, and, except for a few springs and wells, waterless. It must have always been like this, because there is no evidence that any settlement existed here in archaic Greece, and it is quite likely that it was uninhabited until the thirteenth century.

The first settlers seem to have been Balkan shepherds and their families who had grown tired of being killed, raped, and pillaged in their own land. Here they set up a little pastoral community, but because of the poor grazing and lack of water they were obliged to build up a subsidiary seafaring community to make and man boats so that livestock and produce could be ferried across to the mainland and basic stores brought back for the maintenance of the little band of expatriates. Inevitably the seafaring community became of much greater importance than the descendants of the shepherd pioneers: so much so that by the end of the eighteenth century this island was, to Greece and the Eastern Mediterranean, what Devon had been to Elizabethan England.

The island's armed merchantmen — brigs, barques, and brigantines — small, fast, sturdy ships all built in the island's own fortified shipyards, had become something of a Mediterranean legend.

Now, at this time, the Napoleonic Wars broke out and rule of the seas around Europe was being sharply contested by the British fleet under Nelson and the French fleet under Villeneuve; a double blockade of continental Europe. It was a chance that the island seamen seized with gusto. They sailed their armed ships up into the Black Sea and filled them with Russian wheat, then ran it across the Mediterranean for sale or barter to the highest bidder — French, Spanish, Italian, it didn't matter which. If gold was not available, the captains were quite happy to take in payment what is still nicely referred to as *pragmata* — *things* — furniture, statuary, works of art, antiques, church *ikons* (provided, of course, that they were gold), and even bands of skilled artisans who could help them build and decorate the great houses they were erecting in their home port with the profits accrued from their adventuring.

In a matter of no more than five or six years the island had been transformed from a quite unimportant little community of shepherds-gone-to-sea into a stronghold of merchant princes so fabulously wealthy that they didn't know what to do with their money, except to build bigger and finer houses and import more treasures to fill them.

What has always struck me as rather nice about the story is that it is a rare example of a *nouveau-riche* community spending its wealth with faultless good taste; and also, I suppose, an instance of war profiteering which one cannot really condemn.

In appearance, the town today must be almost exactly what it was in the days of its merchant princes, for practically no houses have been built in the last one hundred and twenty years. It rises in tiers around the small, brilliant, horseshoe-shaped harbour — old stone mansions harmoniously apricot-coloured against the gold and bronze cliffs, or washed pure white and shuttered in palest grey: houses austere but exquisitely proportioned, whose great walls and heavy arched doors enclose tiled courtyards and terraced gardens. The irregular tiers are broken everywhere by steep, crooked flights of stone steps, and above the tilted rooftops of uniform red tiles rise the octagonal domes of the churches and the pierced and fretted verticles of marble spires that might have been designed by Wren. Above the town the mountains shoot up sheer, their gaunt surfaces unbroken except for an odd white mill or two, a field of grain standing on end, a dark patch of fir-trees, and three monasteries, the highest of them so close to heaven that at night its lights are looped among the stars.

The ruin of the merchant princes was on the same grand sweeping scale as their rise. In 1820 the island was the richest part of Greece. By 1830 it was bankrupt. In between was the war of liberation from the Turks, and to this cause the island gave grandly of everything it had — its wealth, its ships, its admirals, its captains, its seamen. Of the great naval heroes of Greece most of the greatest came from this one small port. It comes as something of a surprise to realise that there were factors other than Lord Byron in the struggle for Greek independence, but I know now that without the ships and captains of this island it would never have been achieved at all.

The island went down the steep ramp of decay with pride and dignity. About the middle of last century there was a renaissance when it became the centre of the Greek sponge-diving industry, and while this also produced a second merchant aristocracy of wealth, it was comparatively short-lived, and the decline of the island has continued steadily until now. At its most flourishing period it supported a population of more than 30,000: now there are less than 3,000 people living here — supported still by their seamen, who go on adventuring now as captains, mates, stewards, or deckhands in all the merchant ships of Greece.

Dazzled a little by the beauty of the town, one does not realise at first that half the houses are uninhabited. Behind beautiful façades are only desolate weed-choked courts and fallen rafters; and what at first appear to be gaps of virgin mountain rock among the terraces usually reveal themselves — by a piece of carved marble, a Turkish inscription, a tarnished bronze door-knocker lying among the stones — as the foundations of great houses, tiers of houses, terraces of houses, hundreds of houses, long since sunk back to their elements.

On winter nights when the wind whines I find myself listening for the last wild scream of the wrenched shutter, the last sad groan of the subsiding wall, as another house returns, stone to stone and dust to dust, from which it was first so proudly made.

5

This house we have bought is not one of the grand houses of the island. Would that it were. But after three months of panting up and down steps, through lanes and arches and arches and alleys, into courtyards and out, in the wake of the ever-optimistic and tireless Socrates, we were forced into the realisation that the cost of restoration put all the marvellous ruins out of our reach, and although the really big houses in a reasonable state of repair were astonishingly cheap they were still too expensive for us. It was a sad, shocked day when it dawned on us that when a man here talks in terms of pounds he doesn't mean scraps of paper: he means *gold*.

Ours is in the second category of island houses; that is to say, not the house of a merchant-prince or renowned admiral, but of a prosperous sea-captain. It lies in the village behind the waterfront, beyond the little church of St Constantine and below the crag where the Down School is perched so impossibly Up. It occupies one side of a small cobbled square, in the centre of which is a well of rather brackish water, reputed never to run dry.

The square is typical. The side opposite the house is composed of a high stone wall in a bad state of disrepair, behind which lies the partly cultivated garden where the donkeys of Dionyssos the dustman are stabled. On the right is a low building of a charming hexagonal shape that may once have been a tavern or store. Now it is unoccupied, and rather melancholy with its paintless shutters closed and its splotched and peeling walls sprouting long trails of caper flowers among the scrawled legends of village children's play. The left side of the square is occupied by the abandoned lower floor of a house whose top storeys evidently fell in many years ago: it is used as chicken-run, garbage-dump, and wash-line area for its neighbouring house, a pretty place where tubs of flowers line the courtyard and bunches of oranges hang over the wall.

Our inspection party approached from the waterfront. At the foot of the lane that turns up past the Tiliakos restaurant we met the three Swedes, buying cabbages from a moored caique. Their names go something like Rulf and Gulf and Tulf, but George and I privately call them Pepsin, Strepsin, and Amylopsin, The Pancreatic Juices. So impossibly tall they are, so tenderly young, with their three golden tassels of beard gleaming silkily in the sunlight, they look like selected stalks of corn from a bumper crop. On learning our destination they all bowed politely and clicked their heels and requested permission to accompany us.

'We are interesting in the architecture,' Pepsin growled softly from his great height as they arranged their cabbages and fell into line beside us.

'*Werry* interesting,' Strepsin assured us, bending over his particular cabbage to come down within talking range.

'You will please to give us the short history of the so unusual architecture of this island.' Amylopsin's big blue eyes were childlike and trusting. 'I like it most well.'

For the history of island architecture we directed them to Creon, who was marching ahead of us up the lane with quick, short, aggressive steps, his hands thrust deep in his overcoat pockets, his head pushed forward, battering his way through whatever concentration of invisible forces sought to impede his progress. Ursula clung to his side, still bedevilling him about houses.

Strepsin, Pepsin, and Amylopsin strode gigantically forward, and with their three figures swaying deferentially above him — woolly caps, scarlet shirts, cabbages, and all — Creon led on up the lane.

Past the small shop, now open and busy with workmen, where our wicked old Athenian friend Black John is to open a bank in the summer if we can keep him out of Katsikas' Bar, or he can keep his backers ignorant about the glasses of *mastika* filled and clandestinely waiting behind every round of cheese and every flour bin in every store along the waterfront. Past the gnarled, grey fingers of the wistaria vine, already pricked with purple, that clutch and curl around the narrow door of Chloe's house, empty now until summer, when Chloe will come again, a strange, gentle girl who spends inexplicably lonely summers here, painting gentle pictures of houses and boats and shells. Past the dark cooper's shop that I love for the smell of the oak shavings and the great pale curves of barrels caught in burnished bands. Past the rusty tracery of high iron gates that open on to a noble court and a graceful, arched building that was once the town market and now houses the island's temperamental electricity plant and ice factory. Past the shoemaker's window hung all about with good rough shepherds' shoes soled solidly with motor tyres, and nasty plastic sandals from Piraeus.

Past the carpenter's, the oil store, the hot, odorous cavern of the bakery where the women were just emerging with round tin dishes of potatoes and marrows brown from the oven and already congealing in the cooking fat. Past the delicate fanned windows of the long, low church of St Constantine.

And all the women stopped in their doorways to watch us pass.

'When will it be, Kyria?' Archonda the sempstress came into the lane to pat my belly inquisitively.

'Three weeks — four — five. God knows, not I.'

'Good freedom, lady.' The woman called the wish formally, their expert eyes appraising the curve of my coat. Old Kyria Kali — Mrs Good — whom Creon says was the local procuress in the wild old days when the port was wealthy, threw up her hands and shrieked in startled revelation.

'Mother of God! Is it this skinny one in trousers who is having the child then? *Panaygia mou!* I thought it was this other — the *Espanola!*'

Sean let out a shout of laughter as the old woman grabbed Lola and began to prod her professionally.

'These bloody *Greeks!*' Lola muttered indignantly, struggling to free herself. Sean hooted. Kyria Kali squeezed and kneaded. Lola turned, angrily straightening her clothing. The old woman shot out a claw and nipped Lola's bottom so hard that she gave a shriek of real pain, and Kyria Kali collapsed on a doorstep, hugging herself under her shawl in an ecstasy of delight.

'Eeeh! You're a lucky man, young fellow. Long life to you, and a hundred children. Your woman is a fine plum!'

And so we came at last to the house by the well.

Childishly, I tried by closing my eyes and opening them quickly to take the house by surprise. It still looked the same — a square, white block with a heavy peeling door flanked by two small, barred windows, and above them the three tall shuttered windows of the second floor. The third floor, invisible from the front, sits low back behind the roof terrace where once the captain's wife fired off two small cannons on sighting his ship entering port.

Amylopsin said he liked it most well.

The key is a huge mediaeval instrument that weighs two pounds nine ounces. It fits the side entrance, a double wooden gate with a rather nice knocker, very rusty now, of a woman's head crowned with grapes and leaves. I want to find one of the graceful hands that are used as door-knockers on most of the old houses in the village: there is one that I have seen on a ruined house in the upper levels that is a most beautiful thing — a plump, green-bronze hand poised delicately in a bronze lace cuff, the fingers lightly holding a round, red apple. But that is for later, when a windfall is blown our way or the mail brings something more tangible than an editor's comment that he isn't looking for that particular sort of story just at the moment.

The side gate opens on to a small courtyard paved with the pink stone that is quarried on a small satellite island in the gulf, and a flight of broad pink stone stairs that leads to the first floor.

Creon shook the old splintering door experimentally.

'I have decided that this will be your main entrance, George,' Creon said at last. 'You will have a Yale lock for it. Remind me to instruct Dinos to obtain one from Piraeus.'

'But —' I began, my fingers clutching the wonderful huge key.

'The ground floor you will not require at all. Close it off! I shall instruct Dinos.'

'Come and see,' I whispered to Ursula and Lola. We left Creon on the steps arranging and noting instructions while we crawled one after the other through a door so small that it could have been built only for a dwarf.

'It's *my* little door!' squealed Shane ecstatically, wriggling after us. 'It's mine and Martin's and B's when he's born.'

'He'll be born any minute, my love, if your mother uses that door again,' said Ursula.

Crouched in the little square hole, Strepsin and Pepsin peered down wonderingly over their cabbages and sketchbooks, like two Neanderthal Men deciding upon a new lair.

The ground floor is, in fact, a semi-basement, cut down deeply into the island rock to make a great storage cistern for rainwater collected on the upper terrace. Above the cistern there are three rooms, all on different levels and connected by low, wide arches. The floors are grey stone flags, worn silk smooth, the ceilings huge rough beams. Double doors like those of a fortress open out on to the garden, as yet a wilderness of nettles and fallen vines.

'But why do you want to close it off?' Lola asked. 'You must paint it all some lovely mad colour —'

'It *is* a mad colour,' Sean murmured sadly, crawling in to join us.

'Henry. Charmian insists on closing off this bottom floor! Tell her she's out of her mind.'

'What? What are you talking about?' George asked in bewilderment; and Pepsin, peering curiously into a cupboard that gave out a rank odour of mouse-droppings, said plaintively, 'But it is the *history* of the architecture I am interesting in.'

Henry, having discovered an ancient set of dentures on the ledge of the window embrasure, was curled up in a trance, snapping the grinning teeth in one hand, and regarding with a sweet, contemplative smile the mildewed green walls rising out of little symmetrical mounds of powdered plaster and cat dirt, and the receding musty caverns through the arches.

'Best like this, isn't it?' he said. 'When the consummation can be achieved with a thought, with a blink of your eyes, and the vision is still without fault — safe under your skull. I'd like you to have one of my paintings for this wall — if it doesn't wreck the vision, that is?'

'Yes, please,' I said gratefully. 'An Icarus if you can spare one. I'd like Icarus aspiring on that wall.' God knows, I thought, a little aspiration was needed somewhere about!

'I would close it off. I would indeed!' Creon said truculently, bulging his eyes at me while he dusted cobwebs from his sleeve. 'Although ... follow me now!' He bustled into the next room, where a battered tin bucket on a frayed rope hung by the marble well-shaft. 'Here! Here is where you will put the pump.'

'Pump. What pump?' George asked blankly.

'You must have a *pump*, mustn't you? Do you intend to carry buckets of water by hand to the bathroom?'

'But there isn't a bathroom,' said George.

'You will construct one. Follow me and I will show the room which is to be converted. I shall also instruct Dinos to enlarge this entrance. And to remove that old ladder,' he added sternly, glancing through into the kitchen. 'You have no use for it.'

'But it has most much of character,' offered Amylopsin earnestly. 'I like it most well.'

'You forget my godson, sir.' Creon's bulging eyes censured his approval. 'We cannot risk having him fall down ladders. No. I shall instruct Dinos to remove it.'

'Look,' George whispered anxiously, 'for Christ's sake steer Creon away from bathrooms. He'll have a gang of workmen here tomorrow pulling the whole place down and rebuilding it. We can't afford a *bathroom*!'

'Of course you must have a bathroom,' said Henry.

'We can't afford it, I tell you!'

'What the hell does that matter? Have it anyway.'

Just at that moment the courtyard gate flew open wildly, to admit pell-mell a dozen women who had been leaning on it, trying to see through the keyhole. And behind them Hippolyte, jerseyed smartly in grey and yellow stripes and carrying a spray of almond blossom between his fingers.

'Isn't it *heavenly*,' he breathed, waving it at us. 'Oh, after *you*, madame. Yes, if you please. And after you too, mademoiselle. I only want drapes now to feel like Isadora Duncan. Are you all having a party in this nice place?' He looked at us sweetly, his long lashes lowered. 'I didn't mean to intrude, you know, but this bevy of beauties swept me along up the lane. They appeared to think this was the place I ought to be going.'

'It is! Join in! Join in!' George invited. 'Mr Creon Stavris is on top of the stairs there leading an inspection party over this charming residence. I am sure he would be delighted if you would join us. The more the merrier. And you, also, ladies. One and all! I have no doubt you will all be intensely interested in the improvements and alterations he will explain to you now, and which he plans to effect in the very near future.'

'George,' Ursula warned, 'you're becoming overwrought.'

The crowd that now thronged the first-floor rooms was enough to make anyone overwrought, and there were more pouring in through the gate, herding eager children before them. The three golden beards of Pepsin, Strepsin, and Amylopsin made a little scalloped fringe over the terrace wall as they gazed down intently upon the gathering assembly. Above the exclamatory heads of the wheeling women, Hippolyte's branch of almond blossom scattered showers of pale petals. Through it all stalked Creon, arranging bathrooms.

'Perhaps,' George said gloomily, 'it would be better if you and I came back some other day — out of visiting hours.' And he sank down on the top step and rested his chin on his hunched knees. Hippolyte's classic head appeared in a top-floor window.

'Do impress upon Monsieur Stavris that there must be *no* furniture!' he called. 'Perhaps one black bed with brass knobs, and a bead curtain for the hoo-ha. He can sit on a little woven mat to receive guests. Don't you think?'

'Don't worry about the furniture,' George called back. 'There will be one double-bed spring, one mattress for a single-bed, a nursery table, and two Tibetan prayer-wheels. The effect will be spacious.'

'Oh, is it *your* house?' asked Hippolyte in some surprise.

'I don't know any longer.' George rose slowly and took my hand in his and led me on tiptoe down the stairs and out the side gate and into the lane. Very gently he closed the gate behind us, kissed me, and we walked off quietly down the lane to the port.

There was an asbestos caique warping in, most curiously, and charmingly, named *Metamorphosis.*

March

I

Now it is the end of March and the baby still unborn, for which I am glad enough until we see what repercussions will result from the abduction by the British of Archbishop Makarios. Rumours in the *agora* are wild and impassioned. Although all our Greek friends hasten to assure us that we are in high standing in the community and in no danger of being expelled from the country, we, with the rest of the foreign residents, have been summoned quite peremptorily to the police three or four times in succession.

Actually, not one of us is English, but Henry has been asked to produce proof that he is an artist, and Sean's application for a year's extension to his permit has been curtly refused: he has been given only a month. We are worse than uneasy, penniless as we are, and with the imminent drama of birth overshadowing all other fears.

Martin reports rather worriedly that at school now the headmaster makes rousing speeches against the perfidious English, and that the children are all learning ENOSIS songs. Poor little M. gets very pink and uncertain, remembering his English friends, and at the same time yearns for the right to be valorous. We have tried to sort it out for him, but perhaps it is too much to expect that an eight-year-old boy should achieve a state of neutrality while his friends are pinning revolutionary emblems on their school smocks and planning great deeds of bravery. Shane, at seven, hasn't the faintest notion of what it is all about, but responds characteristically to the atmosphere of excitement. She is reported to have been seen leading chanting bands of children through the back streets, shouting Cyprus catchcries and death to the English with every appearance of intense enjoyment.

Perhaps as a courteous act of reassurance to us, or perhaps only because he really has done very well at school this term, Martin was chosen to carry a laurel wreath in the twenty-fifth of March procession, which celebrates Greek independence, and to recite a poem on the monastery steps beside the tomb of the island hero. We stood among the crowd in the courtyard to watch him. Both he and Shane seem to be loved quite genuinely by the islanders: it occurred to me again that in Greece children are one's best insurance policy.

Still, a basic and deep-seated disquiet continues to trouble us, intensified probably by the fact that the weather has turned really cold again.

The wind howls at gale force for days on end, or comes in furious gusts or volleys that create havoc among loose tiles and shutters. The almond trees are stripped of their blossom, the gardens hammered flat. The last of the old Turkish bridges is smashed down, and torrential rains have washed half the mountain soil down the cobbled streets and into the harbour. The Street of the Heroes that leads from the waterfront all the way to the Sweet Wells is feet deep under silt. It is sometimes only possible to get to the *agora* by taking off one's shoes and socks and wading knee deep, and the *agora* itself is usually deserted. All the fruit and vegetable stalls have been taken inside the shops. One swoops along leaning on the wind, and all the way across the gulf the sea peaks and hummocks with wrathful wave-caps. March, in Greece, is the month that put the old woman in the pot.

The children were wildly excited to find snow on the mountain slopes just above the highest levels of the town. They brought it home packed in cardboard boxes and made a little dirty snowman who melted away in sad rivulets across the courtyard while they were gone to find more snow. Only my great belly prevented me from joining them, and the fact that at the time I was fully employed in trying to dry off the family's wet clothes.

34

In the rooms where we live while we get our own house in order we have no other heating than a three-legged tin filled with charcoal embers — very Greek. We huddle over it, planning ceramic stoves and Turkish copper braziers for next winter, when we shall be settled, oh so comfortably, with our own house and good warm clothes for everyone and a reassuring sum of money in the bank. Thank God the delights of anticipation never pall on us: some of the very pleasantest hours I can ever remember have been spent crouching over the charcoal tin, planning courtyards, sailing-boats, making summer trips to islands yet unseen, even while I am engaged on unpicking the children's four-year-old coats and making them up again on the other side of the material so that they, at least, might look reasonably respectable.

Twice this month our island has been cut off from all communication for days on end. Even the Athens steamer could not get close enough to land mail or passengers and was forced to flee for shelter along the mainland coast, where it battled up and down for two days until the sea calmed sufficiently for the captain to risk the open water and the run back to Piraeus.

Secretly I find this very dramatic and exhilarating, even though the impossibility of the market caiques getting through to the island makes our diet pretty dreary at times. We are reduced to lentils, beans, and split peas, with an occasional haunch of stringy goat's meat to add variety. Lola, a fabulous and resourceful cook, throws up her hands sometimes, but managed on Sean's birthday which coincided with one of the famine periods — to produce a dinner which would have done credit to a Cordon Bleu. Her cooking is her one real vanity, and I go to her humbly to learn her miraculous tricks of making pies without ovens, omelettes with one egg, cakes out of stale bread crumbs, or good curries from a piece of old goat's meat and a handful of lentils. One wonders, with awe, of what she might not be capable given a real stove and a choice of ingredients.

Ursula has made it all the occasion to point out to me that if the seas continue so wild I am going to find myself in a desperate

35

plight if the birth of the baby is complicated in any way and it is necessary to take me off to Athens.

This is a fear grown so familiar to me that I am able to pooh-hoo it with every appearance of unconcern. Indeed, at times, I am so filled with vanity at my own interesting and dramatic situation that I indulge myself with secret scenes wherein I die in a terrible and bloody agony that still, however, leaves me capable of making a calm and compelling death-bed speech to George. He, of course, is to marry again for the sake of the children, preferably a Greek girl with a satisfactory dowry — I think I probably have Chloe in mind. At other times I hover over my own funeral cortege toiling up the mountain path among the rocks and olives: I derive a great deal of melancholy satisfaction from the chanting priests and the passing bell, and myself stretched out among the flowers as stiff and white as a freshly pulled garlic stalk.

I notice, however, that I am always a witness to these scenes. Death remains a dramatic concept that my ego refuses to believe in at all. Only at night sometimes, when the harsh lunatic cry of a donkey wakes me, or the child hurts me as it stretches and turns, do I lie staring into the disquieting dark, trapped in the terrible prison of my own body and filled with a fear that is bleak and desolate and *real*. Like the veriest worried girl desperately counting her fingers as the month passes, I babble incoherently that age-old prayer of women: Let me off, please, Lord! Let me off this time and I'll never do it again!

While food is so short we often find it convenient to eat our evening meal at Spiro's restaurant on the waterfront. We are always sure of finding Ursula and Henry, for although Ursula seldom appears in the port in daytime — finding it more comfortable in this beastly weather to send Henry for supplies while she lies in her bed reading Proust or writing her interminable letters to people who might possibly be useful — she is no cook at the best of times and would go supperless during this bitter period were it not for the port restaurants.

Often the Donovans are there too, drawn from their little wind-lashed house on the clifftops by the lights and the company and the long, impassioned arguments around the soiled tablecloth in Spiro's window seat under the Fix beer advertisement.

Sometimes Vassilis the crippled sponge diver joins in, or Tzimmy the pedlar, with his Benghazi basket filled with dead men's clothes. Vassilis sings, stretching wide the gaping hole of his mouth over two yellow teeth that look like the temple at Corinth; the young labourer Apostoli sings to the plaintive accompaniment of his guitar: in dark corner the old men sing, quaveringly and off-key. And sometimes we sing too — folk songs half-remembered or the nostalgic dance tunes that date our love days.

But mostly we talk, individually, severally, and at last all together, hurling and snatching at creeds, doctrines, ideas, theories, ranging through space and time like erratic meteorites rushing on in the full spate of our ignorance as to either our origins or destinations, until at last we come to the blazing point of exhaustion.

The old men have all gone home. Gregorio the cook can no longer smile his affectionate, uncomprehending smile from behind the saucepans grown cold over the grey charcoal ash. The boy Christos pillows his sweet downed face on folded arms across the counter, still with one tired black eyebrow quirked in attention, even in sleep. Ursula, who has long since given up bickering at Henry to take her home, yawns and yawns as she hunches down into her coat and broods on the masts tossing wild in the whining darkness outside the steaming window, and the ludicrous marble lion crouched pale and simpering in the square at the foot of that remote, far-gazing admiral who weathers all storms with disdain.

We pay the reckoning chalked up on the slate, and go our various ways through a stampeding or exploding universe of our own invention, through matter that we have talked into becoming a sort of visible motion, each in his own way feeling pleasantly triumphant — the pessimists having proved to their own satisfaction that life is an irremediable disaster, the optimists hugging to themselves the sweet certainty of the value of existence.

2

Early in the month, while I was still capable of making a long walk, we again climbed across the mountain to the house where Ursula and Henry are staying — a wonderful, twenty-room mansion loaned to them by a wealthy Greek who is an admirer of Henry's painting.

It was built in the period of the island's greatest prosperity on a wild mountain slope overlooking the gulf, and the owner has recently added a bathroom with flush toilet and beds with inner-spring mattresses to the charms of lofty rooms, fine carved furniture, and rare carpets.

I think that Ursula can't quite believe her luck yet. A bathroom again! Tiled stoves and carpets! A real studio for Henry! After all the years of stumbling in Henry's wake through an endless succession of shoddy furnished flats, European hotel rooms, cheap *pensiones*, and the guestrooms of friends, it must seem incredible luxury.

No wonder she hates to leave it. In between Proust and letter writing she is indefatigably tearing up the old neglected garden that surrounds the house so that she might at last begin on her ambitious project of replanting with forget-me-nots, sweet alice, and various other herbaceous plants which she has ordered in seed from England. It seems sad that none of these flowers are likely to thrive on a mountain rock through a parching summer, so that even this, her one real longing to be creative, is almost certain to end perversely in destruction.

As we came over the last rise, through the ruined tiers of houses built like forts or palaces, this house on the mountainside seemed indeed very beautiful. Within the great protecting walls pink vapour puffs of almond blossom wafted down over five stepped terraces to the very doors of the square, white dwelling whose foundations rise sheer from the mountain gorge.

The view from the house-terrace is breathtaking. 'Like a Book of Hours,' Ursula said, climbing painfully down from the high garden where she had been uprooting some innocent wild bulbs that offended her, and pointing with an air of proprietorship at three conical bronze hills crowned each with a single tree, and two white oxen plodding before a plough that sliced curling chocolate grooves among the silver olives. But I must turn again to the sweep of the blue gulf below, the jagged peaks of the islands breaking the foam, and the far dim dream of the mountains of Arcady.

In the studio Henry had spread out his winter's work for inspection: five hundred small sketches in oil paint on the stiff white sheets of heavy art paper that he buys in bundles of a thousand at a time.

The islands are there, the rocks, the goats, the spikes, the thorns — Greece actual. But most of the studies are concerned with Greek myth, browbeaten into tractability. Icarus occurs again and again. The same haunting naked figure soars above fanged rocks and wide, dark seas, sometimes just rising from the ground, sometimes a speck floating high against a burning ball of sun, frail as a dragonfly. And always on the ground, earthbound and staring upwards with sorrowful yearning eyes, is the lonely figure of the Minotaur — a man's body with a bull's head with the wide tapering horns curled upward and the formalised white flower of Crete blooming fresh between his sad human eyes.

There are shields too — whole patterns of them: barbaric things with barbaric legs and arms and eyes and heads entangled with them. Stark and bitter Greeks and Trojans these, dying by Scamander not like heroes but like men, before the Age of Iron, before the stories and the songs. Only the naked horses' heads are godlike.

The sketches are terribly impressive. It occurred to me, not for the first time, that Henry might well turn out to be one of the really important artists. It is not only that galleries are buying his work — galleries as widely spread as the New York Museum of Modern Art, the Tate, the Sydney National Gallery — nor that critics devote a lot of space to appraisals of his strong, strange, vigorous style, nor even the more and more frequent appearance in the erudite monthlies and quarterlies of completely incomprehensible articles that set the seal of success on Henry by losing him completely in a lot of nonsense.

More than all this, one feels the certainty of Henry himself. He knows how good he is. Tiptoeing cautiously between the sheets laid out on the studio floor, one had a queer, secret, and rather shamed, compulsion to touch him for luck.

His face was flushed and his eyes very bright when we sat down to lunch.

'And now what?' asked George.

'Well,' with a sidelong glance at Ursula, 'Paris, I think. For a while.'

'No,' said Ursula. 'I won't. This time I won't.'

'There's a man in Paris who can teach me welding,' said Henry. 'I must learn welding before I can try some of these things in metal!'

'No,' said Ursula, 'I won't. This time I won't. You promised, Henry. You know you did. We have just enough money to buy a house of our own here, and you know you said yourself you have a whole year's painting in front of you. If we spend it going to Paris we won't be able to buy a house at all.'

'Yes,' said Henry, 'but you see this man is so terribly good, and I can *see* these bloody things, you know, clanging away. They won't clang for me in paint. You know how it is when —'

'And where are we going to *live* in Paris?'

'Oh, I don't know,' Henry said in surprise. 'How about that woman you met in Italy? Didn't she say she could always put us up if we came to Paris? Or I suppose we could go to Monique again. We know lots of people in Paris.'

'No!' said Ursula.

'Oh, but we'll be back at the end of this year. We'll buy a palace if you like, with walls fifty feet high and ten acres of garden.'

'No!' said Ursula. 'I won't go, Henry. I won't.'

Henry laughed. 'She's always worrying about money. Look, old girl, money is something to *use*, not to worry about. Between now and the end of the year, I bet you I'll sell six paintings.'

'You mean that *I* will have to sell six paintings.'

'All right! That's the girl! We'll have a fine time in Paris, you'll see.'

'I'm not going to Paris. I'm damned if I go a step further with you.'

'Ah yes.' Henry laughed still, patting her hand. 'And when we come back I'll buy you a house. We'll have a house with a great big cellar where I can have a forge. Did you ever see the cellar in this house?' he asked George. 'It's the most wonderful bloody studio ever. You can't see out of it *at all!*'

And Ursula, staring grimly out of the window at three bronze hills and a sweep of stormy water, turned and cried across the room in a shrill voice of despair, 'I hope you two know how lucky you are!'

There is an echo of this in a letter from London, which chronicles a horror story from George's former office with a faintly accusative note that is becoming familiar:

'It's all very well for you lucky ones lazing by the Mediterranean!'

'Fortune's *darling!*' says George coyly, relieving me of the bellows and charcoal so that I may sort through the lentils for the stones and black beetles that always make up a quarter of the weight.

And later, draping wet coats and sodden jerseys in a circle around the charcoal tin, 'Perhaps I could peel you a lotus?'

All the same, he is inevitably buoyant after such a letter, needing occasionally just such a reminder of the sterility and frustration of his former materially successful life to confirm his decision never to return to it.

At least our way of life is of our own choosing. We even derive some peculiar satisfaction from our discomforts as we become more aware that we are learning again the true values of light and warmth and food and shelter, which for so many years we have taken for granted. Sometimes it seems to me that this is a sort of educational programme from which one day we might graduate qualified to live our lives with better understanding.

Both of us are inclined to set up arbitrary staging posts in time, and gallop towards them at a furious pace, always hopeful that beyond the post the prospect will open out pleasant and fair. Now it is 'when we move into the house', and 'when the baby is born', two points of arrival that have a special significance by being coincidental. I invariably arrive at my staging posts in a mixture of exhaustion, relief, triumph, and brimming hopefulness: by the time I have seen that the path ahead is as difficult as ever I have already set up another post, and can gallop on towards it as hopefully as ever. No disappointments seem to cure me of this.

'When we move into the house' glimmers golden ahead, gateway to a time of felicity when the sun will shine, my waistline be slender, the post bring cheques from appreciative editors, the children stop picking their noses, the Greek language reveal itself as simple after all, our writing problems be solved, and we shall all live together in harmony and contentment like a little tribe which has at last reached the Promised Land.

We are rushing on to this point willy-nilly, in a sea of cement and pipes and pumps and steel girders.

Creon has taken over. Nothing we can say can stop the fever of activity mounting daily in the house by the well. Any doubts we might have had about committing ourselves to the expense of a bathroom have been completely overruled, less, I think, by Creon's insistence than by our own secret yearnings for something more advanced than the tin dish and the tray of Benghazi sponges that have served for our ablutions for nearly two years now. And it has been all too easy to listen to Henry's attractive argument that in this life you must take what you want and think about paying for it later. He is vehement in this: it is an article of faith with him.

So in a moment of surrender so reckless that we dare not think of it we have allowed Creon to order from Athens a square porcelain shower tray and wash-hand-basin with a wonderful swivelling tap, and a gleaming white toilet bowl whose tank is labelled 'The Best Niagara'.

Unfortunately there seems to have been a mishearing somewhere of the instructions that George, in his not-very-good Greek, gave to Dinos — with the result that we have not one flush toilet, which would be rare enough in this part of the world, but *two*. One is inside the house and one is outside, and both have been tiled with imported German tiles costing four *drachmae* apiece. We dare not count them. And as they are firmly cemented into the walls we cannot very well ask Dinos to remove them.

I found him looking at George with a sort of qualified pride, as if he is quite pleased with the way things have turned out but not at all sure whether he will ever be paid for his labours. The doubt is mutual, but I am glad to say that George did not betray this.

The team of workmen under Dinos — the youngest of whom is aged about seven — have also been engaged in fixing a huge galvanised water tank to the back wall of the tank about thirty feet above the level of the cistern; this is the key to the hydrocloacic system which is to make our house the envy of the island.

George is a little nervous about this too, since he has discovered that the tank has a capacity of one cubic metre and that he, as the man of the house, will be expected to pump by hand one ton of water up those curling pipes every time the tank needs filling. The pump is a Heath Robinson device, most cheerfully blue.

To cut down on expenses a little (ridiculous crotchet when one calculates — or, rather, determinedly does not calculate — the money represented by every chaste gleam of the German tiles and the number of *drachmae* that rightfully will be expected by those ten great sweating men swarming up ladders and through windows and being ostentatiously worthy of their hire) we have decided to paint the three ground-floor rooms ourselves. There is a sense of urgency behind this. I am still obsessed by the notion to have my baby born in my own house.

'But we can't possibly have the whole house ready,' George says worriedly. He is willing to humour me, but frenzied already at the number of things to be done before the house is even habitable.

'One room then,' I reply implacably.

'But suppose you *start* round at the other house or in the street or somewhere,' Lola suggests, with a personal and rather nervous interest. She has promised to come and ward off the Greek ladies who will consider it their hereditary and inalienable right to scurry to a room of confinement like rats to an unguarded rubbish tin. Lola has majesty and presence enough to cope with them. Besides, she can swear like a navvy when roused, in French, English, Spanish, and even Greek.

'Wherever I start,' I say firmly, 'I shall remove myself, or be removed if necessary, to this house.'

Apart from my private resolution on this point, I have a perverse enjoyment in scaring them all out of their wits. I am so mysterious and terrible to them at the moment, and I feel that this is some slight compensation for the fact that my back hurts and my ribs seem to be permanently displaced and I am heavy with more than the dragging heaviness of the child — sometimes I am scared out of *my* wits too.

'We'll do it for you, sweet,' George says lightly. 'But be a good girl and hold off for as long as you can.'

His face is very drawn and tired, and his eyes, peering out red-rimmed from the splotches of whitewash encrusted on eyebrows and lashes, are anxious for me. I am suddenly ashamed of myself, remembering that the mail has brought nothing for weeks but a gold-bordered invitation to a Hartnell dress show, a circular on the Kashmir Problem emanating from the office of the High Commissioner for Pakistan, and an air letter from an acquaintance of last summer announcing his imminent return to the island. Publishers, agents, editors, all seem to have died, or the ships we sent out so confidently have foundered. From the quarters where our bread and butter is earned there is nothing but silence.

Hold off! Hold off! I scarcely dare to breathe. The workmen shy like startled horses if I set foot on a ladder, and there is a sharp inward hissing of breath every time I lumber through the dwarf door.

They have all been infected by the excitement of the race. They bang and hammer and saw and clatter away, and gallop upstairs and down, with an occasional nervous dark eye cocked at my stomach, as if I might explode in their faces before they can get finished and quit of the house.

The kitchen looks like a sorcerer's cave (there are two small apprentices now, one of whom looks only *six* years of age: I suppose both must be legally of an age to labour twelve hours a day), with somebody for ever stirring up cement in a wooden washthrough, and George, stripped to shorts and streaming with sweat despite the cold, muttering imprecations over an incredibly complicated whitewash formula he is mixing in a kerosene tin.

There is no chance whatever of simplifying the mixture since Creon, dapperly overcoated and wearing a flower in his lapel, stands over the stooped and straining figure of George like a patrician over his slave, making quite sure that his instructions are carried out to the minutest detail.

Through it all Hippolyte drifts rhapsodically, stepping daintily over paint tins, oil rags, bundles of piping, and small, wondering boys. Pepsin, Strepsin, and Amylopsin (who have sold their gold watches and cameras in order to stay on a couple more months) crouch in corners sketching architectural details and asking Serious Questions in their strange, childish, sing-song growly voices, as though George and I are some peculiar abstract theory they must explore before they can get on to the next problem. Their eyes are quite blank and blue and innocent, but beautiful, like the eyes of certain insects, or bits of glass one finds among pebbles on the shore. Their teeth are very white, their tongues virginally pink. Vaguely I am horrified by them, as by Men from Mars.

Lola and Sean come every day. Henry comes, and sometimes Ursula, to watch work in progress, to comment, advise, or just walk from room to room. Transients all, they are experiencing vicariously through us and our house the problems and pleasures of settling down. So they come and go through the day, each according to his mood wistful, envious, thoughtful, irritable, or wearing the lightness of their own unmortgaged freedom like wings.

The women who will be my neighbours come too — Kyria Heleni, Kyria Spirathoula, Little Cuckoo, Kyria Rita, Kyria Metaxaiki — seamen's wives these, menless women, with a high-pitched wail of loneliness underlying their curiosity and excitement and envy like a protracted note of hysteria. Their children, whose age gaps correspond to the duration of foreign voyages, dart in and out, are mislaid in corners and cupboards, hauled down from window-ledges and out of cement heaps, kissed and cuffed alternately with the same pent-up passion. The house at such times is filled with a squawking and chattering and screeching, as though it has become a nesting place for seagulls.

The glories of the bathroom have spread streets away: aunts and cousins and grandmothers are brought to see it. Shane and Martin accept toffees and marbles and plastic *ikons* from an impatient army of children all labouring under the delusion that they are going to be allowed to pull the chain. Shane basks in the special envy of her little girlfriends, and is subject to the fondling of the mothers of sons, for neither Shane nor the mothers doubt that the house is to be part of Shane's dowry. In Greece it is always considered wise to establish connections early.

Daily George becomes more apprehensive about the neighbours.

'It seemed such a *quiet* neighbourhood before we started work on the house,' he one day remarked rather worriedly to Creon.

'Quiet?' Creon pushed his head forward truculently, his grizzled eyebrows making furious triangles on the furrows of his brow. '*Isn't* it quiet?'

'Well, all these damned women, Creon. You know … just walking in and out all day without even knocking. I don't see how we're going to work if —'

'Dismiss it from your mind, George! It is nothing! Absolutely nothing! Why, when Georgaiki was arranging *his* house five women came out of one of the packing cases. They will get used to you in time.'

3

And now the wind pipes away the last mad days of March. George has been appearing and disappearing, laden with string-bags, suitcases, carry-alls, or strung about with kitchen saucepans. 'When we move into the house' is only days away. 'When the baby is born' can also only be days away.

I have been huddled inside over the charcoal tin: apart from the fact that I tend to roll in the wind like a jettisoned barrel it has become embarrassing to walk anywhere in the port.

'When?' call the women from their doorways and windows. 'Haven't you made a mistake?' 'Don't you feel some pains yet?' And Vassilis the sponge diver, sitting out of the wind with his cronies at an iron table around the corner from Soteris' café, opens the gaping pink hole of his mouth and roars delightedly, 'It's waiting for warmer weather!'

Creon is becoming impatient for his godson and no longer troubles to hide his irritation with me: if he thought the child might be a girl I am sure he would wash his hands of the whole business. Ursula is so unnaturally cheerful that I know she is certain of Complications. Lola is nervously jolly, so I suppose that Ursula has been feeding her ghoulish stories as a way of preparing her for what in Ursula's opinion is sure to happen. Even the children say it wasn't fair to tell them about the baby if I intended to wait so long to have it. I am disturbed to find that the goofy dog Max looks at me with a mournful curiosity, as if I have become strange even to him.

Waiting for George to return from the post office, my own weariness with the damned great load of my belly wells up in me, so that as he lunges through the door, looking oddly pale and peculiar, I begin to shout something tearful about jumping down the stairs and getting this baby out of me.

And at this he is paler yet, his lanky body rigidly arrested, his eyes wild, and in a tight, low voice he says that far from jumping down the stairs what I bloody well have to do is to go to bed this very minute and not move a bloody muscle! 'You hold off!' he says fiercely. 'You hold off for all you're worth! I have just met the midwife at the wharf. The last I saw of her she was being rowed out to the Athens boat. She is going to her cousin's wedding in Piraeus!'

'My God! But what did she say?'

'She said *avrio* and *alli evthomada* and *then pirasi*, meaning, I took it, that you wouldn't be ready till *next* week, or else she'd be back next week, and then she waved very cheerfully and got in the bloody boat!' He stops, breathing heavily, and looks at me pleadingly. 'Christ Almighty!' he says. 'There *is* another one, isn't there?'

There is another one. She lives on the mountain and she has long black claws and a hooked beak and brews up little stews of herbs — hemlock, I think. If her name isn't Hecate it ought to be. She cleans down the newborn babies (when she gets them out in one piece, that is) with bundles of used newspaper.

'Well, Ursula then,' says George desperately. 'She used to be a nurse, didn't she?'

'Psychiatric.'

Oddly enough my predominant emotion is one of shame. I wish I could crawl now behind a bush somewhere and just do it quietly all by myself. Somehow I convinced George that there is really nothing to worry about, that I'll hold off all right, and even if I don't it doesn't really matter anyway because, after all, it's a perfectly natural happening, and any woman in the town is competent to deal with it. And soothing him in this way I find that what I am saying is good sense and that I am calm and still and sure of myself, and of him, and of the fundamental rightness of our way of living, and I don't really care a hoot in hell if the midwife gets married herself in Piraeus and never comes back.

4

At night I don't sleep much anymore. Perhaps it is that the wind has dropped at last, and after the electricity plant has shuddered to a standstill at midnight every noise of the night falls separately into a huge black sounding-box of silence.

The weird, agonised cry of a wakeful donkey booms and reverberates, quite close another donkey answers, and the sounding-box is filled with a terrible honking and gasping

48

that wheezes into silence iust as a rooster begins to crow. The roosters are all mad here, nervous, nocturnal birds of splendid plumage and no time sense. And then, while the roosters are tossing their boasts up and down the sleeping terraces, the night is torn by fiendish howls of rage and lust and terror, and those are the island cats who are already so large, so numerous, and so utterly evil that it seems likely they will eventually force the human population to abandon the island to them. Lying in the dark one might be in a jungle.

The house where we are staying has a little terrace tucked under the tall bronze mountain that curls over the town like a static wave. I sit up here wrapped in a blanket, listening to the dialogue of donkeys, seeing shadowed wall, rooftop, tile, alley aswarm with huge slinking shapes of cats, like an emanation of the secret soul of the place.

Athena's little owl drops two liquid notes from the mountain, and again two notes, very pure and chill. Some restless stirring in a high sheepfold is signalled by a little drift of bells. All pale and quiet the lovely houses sleep, tier upon tier folding down from the black bulk of the mountains to the black silk spread of water. Across the water the dark hills of Troezen are pricked all over with the fires of the charcoal burners like a scattering of rubies.

My face is cold turned up to the cold stars. Inexorable and orderly they move across heaven, star beyond star, nebula beyond nebula, universe beyond universe, wheeling through a loneliness that is inconceivable. Almost I can feel this planet wheeling too, spinning through its own sphere of loneliness with the deliberation of a process endlessly repeated, a tiny speck of astral dust whirling on into the incomprehensibility of eternity. How queer to cling to the speck of dust, whirling on and on, perhaps at this moment even upside down. There's no comfort in the stars. Only darkness beyond darkness, mystery beyond mystery, loneliness beyond loneliness.

Wrapped in its own darkness and mystery and loneliness the child in my body turns, as though to remind me of mysteries closer to hand. And I go spinning on through space, enveloped

49

by mystery, enveloping mystery, ignorant as a sheep as to why I am being used in this way. On the dark little terrace under the dark mountains I have a childish desire to shake my fists and shout into the impossible emptiness between those wheeling stars, 'This is all very well, but who am *I*?'

April

I

We have moved house and are feeling suitably triumphant. Even with the four of us cantering from room to room in aimless excitement, followed by the uneasy dog and an army of neighbouring women, the house seems very large and very, very empty. I imagine the ladies are terribly disappointed that we did not arrive with attendant mule trains loaded with plush sofas and veneered sideboards and tasselled tablecloths; but still the bathroom cannot be denied, nor 'The Best Niagara'. On the whole they seem prepared to wait a little before they dismiss us as frauds and mark Shane down low on the list of future brides.

Besides the mounds of cases and bundles awaiting unpacking and disposal, the house is furnished with three beds, a table, four chairs, the long bench George and I use as a desk, and a new wicker basket that is still, thank God, empty. We have also a traditional island settle which we found in an abandoned house. It is rather wormy, the seat is made of planks of driftwood nailed crudely across, and a leg has fallen off. But the back is carved beautifully with urns and garlands, and Tasso the carpenter says he can fix it as new for ten *drachmae* or so.

Creon is sending around six cane chairs and a rather nice Victorian horsehair sofa that he insisted we take from the dank and melancholy warehouse that adjoins the House of Usher, where once a hundred men worked with snicking shears among salty mountains of sponges and great bleaching vats and presses and corded bales — stamped with the names of half the countries of the earth. And Zoë has found a huge old marble-topped farm table, Chloe has sent four ladder-back chairs, Black John is shipping down in a caique from Piraeus various old *pragmata*, including a wonderful round table that will need only some brisk rubbing-up with tan boot polish to achieve genuine antique standing.

Someone has chalked EOKA on our front door, but I suspect Shane. And when the women gathered around the well this evening with their buckets and ropes, Kyrie Heleni dipped the end of her apron in the bucket of well water and carefully washed the sign away.

They say some new foreigners have arrived. Americans, who are looking for a good house to rent for the summer. But the midwife hasn't.

2

The Athens boat comes in just before noon, a small white graceful ship that was once Count Ciano's private yacht and was given to Greece as part of Italian reparations. She still has a *poule de luxe* look, an unequivocal air of luxury and pleasure as she slides through the milky sea with a slow lifting curl of the wake and an insolent tilt to her bows: not all the old black-shawled women screaming and squawking nor the hawking and spitting of the deck passengers can tarnish her gaiety and elegance. She wears bunting by day, and at night she is outlined with strings of tiny fairy lights.

For the fifth day in succession we waited behind the pickets on the waterfront while the rowing boats dipped slowly out to where the *Sirina* was hove-to beyond the headland with its battlements and toy cannons. Above the cannons the island flag curled bravely, fluttering extravagant gold tassels. The tinny strains of a *bouzoukia* band twangled over the harbour.

George chewed his fingernails as he strained to see the passengers dropping clumsily from the *Sirina*'s little ladder into the gently rocking longboats.

Creon walked backwards and forwards behind the pickets with his hands clasped behind his back and his head swaying in a furious baffled sort of way.

I lowered myself with infinite caution onto a chair that was brought me from the Tiliakos restaurant by a scurrying, half-scared small boy who had been curtly summoned by Creon.

The morning gathering of villagers grouped behind the pickets gazed at me with their quick dark eyes, trying to suppress their interest and excitement, longing for drama. I felt a sudden wild elation and wanted to giggle. It was all so very gay and comic — the silly cannons, the oversize and too-gaudy flag, the *bouzoukia* band, the moustaches of the muleteers, the donkeys' decorated saddles and blue bead necklaces, the turkeys trussed for shipment somewhere, Creon pacing up and down, the rowing boats approaching like walnut shells floating on lemonade, the cheerful derisive little toot of the *Sirina*'s whistle, George standing on one leg like a crane, peering at the rowing boats in a parody of anxiety.

Nothing could possibly eventuate from such a scene but a happy ending.

The rowing boats approached one behind the other, dragged slowly across the musical comedy backdrop. George and Creon pushed through the crowd inside the pickets. The duty sailor gravely made way for them on the landing steps.

Then Creon was shouting in a dramatic voice, and George was reaching out his hand to help ashore a floral dress decked with three strings of artificial pearls. The plump red face above the pearls was smiling quite cheerfully and nodding at George. Obviously she was more concerned with the set of her permanent wave.

'New?' I asked, indicating the permanent.

'A hundred *drachmae*. Piraeus.' She smiled at me blithely and her shrewd blue eyes sketched a wink. 'You ought to have yours done after the baby. It makes a woman feel good.'

George hovered behind her, his face parodying relief as it had parodied anxiety a moment before. Creon towered — quite, quite speechless. And the crowd watched with great interest while the midwife stooped and slid her hands professionally under my duffel coat. When she straightened up she hitched down her corset and relieved George of her packages.

'Take the short cut up the stairs behind Kyrios Stavris' house,' she said to him cheerfully. 'And if it's dark bring a torch. The mules use the stairs a lot and I wouldn't want you to slip and break a leg. Even a man is useful when there's a new baby.'

She patted my hand, smiled in a comradely way at George, and limped off down the quay in very new, very tight, and very high-heeled shoes. When she got to Katsikas' she turned and waved — I think to Creon.

George sat down quite suddenly on the landing steps.

'All right, sweetie,' he said. 'You can let go.'

3

And after all it happened very well with me. Athena's little owl dropped its pure separate notes from the mountain, a fringed paring of moon had joined the stars wheeling past my window, the donkeys yearned with fearful honks and gasps.

Before dawn George took the torch and went for the midwife — I can remember the lurching skid of his sandals on the cobblestones as he ran down the lane away from the house, and I can remember the midwife coming and that her hands were very kind, and that instead of the floral dress she wore a big white apron.

There was no need to send for Lola because the neighbouring women were still asleep, and I must have been quiet enough because the children in the next room did not wake. George came in and out with lamps, towels, steaming cans of water; and once somebody else came, another woman in a black dress, and she and the midwife whispered together and then she went away again.

Then it was over and I was lying on a lumpy bed in the grey dawn, an empty body that seemed to be completely out of control so terribly was it shaking and shuddering. The patch of floor I could see looked like a slaughterhouse, but the midwife was still smiling cheerfully as she tilted a bottle of *ouzo* into my mouth — it was delicious, so biting and burning, pouring down my throat and running all sticky over my face and neck.

George's voice was somewhere saying something about a kitten, and Shane was squeaking yes it was a kitten because I heard it, and George said no it wasn't a kitten it was B come at last and B was a boy, and he thought they could see him in a few minutes.

The *ouzo* was still running down my throat and all over my face, and a woman in black, the same one maybe, brushed past the bed with a bunch of dried daisies and there was some talk about fine ground sugar and lemons, and then I knew that I was beautifully, triumphantly, and absolutely drunk.

'She'll be all right now,' the midwife said very matter-of-factly.

I could see her far far away wrapping up a bundle of something and I wanted to see whether it was the baby or fine ground sugar but I was much too drunk, so I closed my eyes and went to sleep.

4

He is a big baby, fair like the other two, with a thick neck and a big, round head and a cry that is deep and angry. When the coast is clear of visiting Greek ladies I like to have his basket beside my bed where I can look at him.

The neighbours run in and out all day, chattering and laughing, bringing little bowls of soup and sticky sweets and bunches of flowers and *ikons* and amulets. Each of them spits three times as she crosses the threshold to ward off the Evil Eye from my room, but for the most part they do it rather furtively, with their heads turned away from me — very much aware, I think, of Lola's dark eyes fixed balefully upon them. Lola doesn't hold with spitting. She throws a blanket right over the baby's basket whenever a step is heard on the stairs.

For all that the baby comes in for a lot of spray, and his basket and blanket are encrusted with *ikons* and amulets and protective medallions, one of which, surprisingly, is an English sixpence strung on a blue ribbon, which was brought in by one of the little seagull nestlings from the house next door. Even old Kyria Kali hobbled in to see me — I think that to the end she really believed it was Lola who was about to give birth: she has been heard to express the gravest doubts concerning my sex and had obviously come to see for herself.

'Mother of God!' she sighed, 'I'm an old woman!' and spat three times on my face and three times on the face of the baby and crossed herself wonderingly and hobbled away.

In spite of my protests, the midwife had swaddled the baby Greek fashion, bandaged him stiff as a board, so it wasn't until she handed over full charge to Lola that George and I could unwind those barbaric wrappings and examine him in detail … the pale, crumpled hands that waved about like starfish, as yet without intelligence, purpose, or will, but scored on each minute palm with the lines that are his own individuality, lines distinct from any other human being on the face of the earth … his wrinkled old man's legs that are still useless appendages to the all-important stomach and shoot up at a touch to settle back into the familiar foetal position with one delicate foot crossed elegantly over the other. His eyes are beautifully blue and swively. He looks more like a tadpole than anything else. The house is filled with an immoderate happiness.

5

This is a time — and perhaps one will need to remember it later — when George whistles a lot, spoils the children extravagantly, gets roaring drunk with the fishermen, grandly hires a caique to take him to the bank on the next island, so that he may withdraw the very last money we have to pay off the workmen and give a celebration dinner in the Tiliakos restaurant for my safe delivery.

He talks of growing a beard, of buying a boat, of taking me to Venice for a holiday. Or leaning on the hoe among the nettles under the lemon tree he talks in a wild spate of words, punctuated with great shouts of laughter and explosions of obscenity, of masters and slaves, of cities and people, of journeys, meetings, partings, triumphs, despairs, frustrations, talks of hope and hopelessness, talks of all the arrivals and all the setting outs, as if his life was a knotted ball that he is madly unravelling backwards ... all the way back to the flat suburban streets and the flat suburban houses behind the safe silver wire fences and the child waiting in the bathroom for his father to enter with the razor-strop to administer the ritual monthly beating. 'For the sins', his father said, 'I have not found out.' Upstairs in the long bare room that will one day be a studio he uses the typewriter as if he were trying to make it talk too.

This is a time when old Mrs Silk comes rapping at our gate with her iron-tipped staff. Every morning at eleven she comes — an obese old woman wearing the old-style bodice and gathered skirt, headscarf, and apron. She has a big wart on her nose and tufts of colourless hair on her chin and ancient steel-rimmed spectacles secured by a piece of pink elastic.

'Health and joy, children!' she shouts, falsely hearty. Her breath is like a blast from a lion's cage: her eyes are narrow and watchful. 'Is Sophia in?'

'She has gone to the market, Mrs Silk.'

'What's that? Gone to the market?' Her voice becomes ingratiating, she wheedles archly with her head on one side and her eyes diamond-hard with suspicion. 'I'll just look for myself now.'

We stand aside while she laboriously hoists herself up the stairs and painstakingly searches through every room, upstairs and down, in cupboards and under ladders, even furtively prodding the mattresses with the end of her staff. She chats in the same ingratiating voice all the time, no doubt to distract us from her purpose.

'Gone to the market, children? Gone to the market? But she said she'd be in.' And wheeling on me suddenly she prods me with her staff. 'You, now! Are you a woman, tell me?'

'Yes, Mrs Silk. Look, here is my baby. And there are my other children up in the school playground.' My shirt is sodden with milk — surely it is all too obvious I am a woman! But old Mrs Silk says 'Ah!' and cackles conspiratorially with her dreadful old face an inch away from mine. 'Where's your skirt, then?' she whispers with her finger to her nose, and while I am still backing away she turns and whips up the lid of a tin trunk.

'Did you say Sophia had gone to the market, now?'

'Yes, Mrs Silk.'

'Well, well,' she says, reluctant, lingering still, so obviously disbelieving. 'You will tell her I called?'

'Yes, Mrs Silk.'

'Then good day to you. Health and joy and long life.' But even at the gateway she makes a final wheedling appeal. 'Isn't Sophia in, now? Tell me, children. She said she'd be in.'

It is sixteen years, Kyria Rita says, since Sophia died in this house ...

This is a time when we try to track down an old island chest to contain our clothes. Neither of us knows the Greek word for 'chest of drawers', but George explains to Little Cuckoo what we want, very carefully and with a multitude of gestures. She appears to understand. She knows a woman who has a very old one. Drawers? George asks again, and pulls imaginary drawers in and out to make quite sure she is clear on this point. Surely, says Little Cuckoo, pulling drawers in and out, lots of drawers. And we *can* put clothes in it? Little Cuckoo shrugs, that maddening Greek shrug that means at one and the same time a denial of all responsibility and 'for God's sake are you really as stupid as all that? Put what you want in it,' she says.

We go to make the inspection in a white house that has geraniums in the courtyard and doves in the cellar — and the chest of drawers turns out not to be a chest at all but a birdcage fashioned with admirable lunacy in Vienna a couple of hundred years ago and brought to the island by some sea captain with a taste for the exotic. It has gables and eaves of intricately fretted wood, gilded, it has lacy doors with minute gold knockers and stained-glass windows that throw flickering flower shadows of purple and red and green and yellow. See all the drawers, says Little Cuckoo, and pulls them in and out to show us where the water goes and the birdseed and the crumbs. It is very old, she adds ... just what you wanted ...

And, of course, it *is* just what we wanted, and what we must have, even if our clothes have to stay in suitcases for another year. It is entirely suitable, says George gravely, and in a quick exchange of raised eyebrows and deprecating gestures, he, Little Cuckoo, and the owner of the birdcage adjust the price to three hundred *drachmae*.

At home we hang it above the well-shaft, where it revolves in a beam of sunlight, spinning delicate shadows of eaves and perches and coloured rosettes. It is a very *gemutlich* article, and I have no doubt that somewhere in the village a *gemutlich* bird, gilded perhaps, with emerald eyes, is waiting in some old sea-chest to be discovered.

This is a time when the crates of books we last saw descending one cold November day into a dank basement in St George's Square, with the fog creeping up from the Thames, are unloaded on the waterfront from a salmon-pink caique with a lemon-yellow waterline and delivered to the house by five very small donkeys wearing bells and blue bead necklaces. There is a touch of the miraculous about it, as if the crates have travelled under some saintly aegis, for the salmon-pink caique is also named St George — *Agios Giorgios*.

With books piled on every window-ledge we are rich again, and there are other things in the crates too: forgotten nursery toys that the children greet with queer little grunts of wonder, unable quite to believe that this treasure is their own; a few good pieces of silver salvaged from the sale of our worldly goods; odd lengths of material apparently packed to fill in corners; concert programmes, documents, letters, photographs, newspaper clippings — what George calls the portable attic. Nostalgic stuff. And two stiff-collared city shirts with a selection of bow ties which we examine with awe. 'For Socrates, do you think?' But George has another suggestion, which is not printable.

This is a time when the mountains of Troezen are crumpled plush, and the sea rings the island in separate strands of blue like embroidery skeins, when the caiques bring fresh vegetables every day, lettuce and spring onions, the first of the cucumbers, the first of the tomatoes, when Johnny Lulu puts out a blue and white awning, when the coffee tables are all moved out from inside the shops on to the cobbles, when Socrates skitters up and down the town trailing a string of coloured flags and shouting a delirious Ya! Ya! to everyone in passing; when old brown men come out from their fusty rooms to blink away mornings on sunny doorsteps, and old grey women tie fresh headscarves over skimpy pigtails and whisk up steaming piles of donkey droppings to nurture spring gardens.

This is a time when Creon issues a warning about removing woollen underwear, and Lola goes out sketching on the mountainsides with Hippolyte, or billows along the quay overflowing spectacularly from a flowered dress that was designed, I think, in days when she was slimmer and frequented smart parties in the *salons* of Madrid ... surely it was never meant to be worn with a shopping basket and shepherd's boots? This is a time when One-Eye, the muleteer, a dour man and one not given to flights of imagination, reports to an entranced audience that as he came down the mountain he saw Ursula stalking stark naked about the terrace with her hair unloosed about her ravaged face and an open book in her hand, disdainful of the hail of whizzing oranges that Henry was hurling at her from a bowl on the parapet. (Ursula says she was only taking her daily sunbath, and Henry explains the oranges away rather sheepishly by saying he was studying trajectories. But, for all that, they are definitely going to Paris.) This is a time when Sean pockets his rejection slips with a grin of gentle self-derision and goes back to his desk. 'Ah well,' he says, 'and sometimes you think you can fly.'

'Fly, then!' says Henry. 'Bloody well soar, why don't you?'

This is a time when I almost have to pinch myself to believe in my own existence, when I walk along the waterfront with my body my own again — how light it feels, how oddly uninhabited — floating just above the cobbles through myriad small radiant explosions of sunlight and an intoxicating geometry of cafe tables, ship's prows, doors, windows, houses, rooftops, rigging, that sing their coloured scraps of arcs and cubes and angles so piercingly as to almost burst my heart. As though it is me who has just been born.

6

'Now,' said the police captain, 'we will write down your name if you please, also the name of your father and mother, your place of birth and date, your marital state and profession, the number of your children. And for your wife also.'

'But you have all that already,' George said. 'It's all there on the passports, and on our residence permits. The sergeant writes it all down every three months.'

'That's regulations,' said the police captain. 'This is different. I have my instructions. Corporal Constantopolis! You get some forms now and fill them in with the Kyrios' particulars.'

'What forms, Captain?' Corporal Constantopolis, a thin, bewildered youth with a faint proud down on his upper lip, looked rather apprehensive.

'Mother of God!' said the captain. 'Well, send out for some coffee, then.'

'Sweet for me,' said Creon curtly. 'Sweet and heavy. And get it from Soteris, mind — not from Dimitri.' Creon was wearing his official face, very stern. 'Now, Captain,' he said briskly, 'let's get on with the business.'

The captain, a sad, heavy man, sighed and rustled a sheaf of old yellowed papers. 'I don't know why you want to live here, Kyrios Giorgios. Just look out the window. Rocks and ruins, that's all this place is.'

'You don't know what you're talking about, man,' said Creon. 'This island was the greatest in Greece.'

'Oh yes.' The captain shrugged disinterestedly. 'Is Australia anything like this, Kyrios Giorgios?'

'No,' said George. 'Not really.'

'It must be a good place then. I have a farm in the Peloponnese. That's a good place too. You don't think you could get an Australian tractor for my farm, do you?'

'No,' said George. 'I don't think so.'

'No? Well then, let's get on with it. What purpose had you in coming to this island, Kyrios?'

'*Kyrie eleison!*' Creon said irritably. 'You know all that! The man is a writer. He wants a place where he can write quietly.'

'Couldn't have picked any place much quieter. Except a cemetery. Just look down the *agora* now. They haven't even heard of the invention of the wheel here yet.' The captain sighed again and shuffled around for another torn scrap of paper under the pile of rubber stamps, dipped his pen in a dry inkwell, swore, and began searching in his pockets. Creon snorted and offered him a fountain pen. The captain tested it on an old dossier. The corporal came back, carrying a round tin tray that swung on three chains from a ring. We sorted out the coffees and all lit cigarettes.

'Now, Constantopolis, sit at your table and prepare to fill in the forms.'

'Yes, Captain, but which forms?'

'Idiot! Don't you know your forms yet? Look, there is a whole cabinet of forms. Take one and write!' He put down his coffee cup, turned again to George, and looked official. 'Now, Kyrios, why do you wish to purchase a house on this island?'

'I don't *wish* to purchase a house,' George said quietly. 'I have *purchased* a house.' His hands were clenching and unclenching on his knees. I gave him a good hard kick under the table.

'What am I to write down, Captain?' asked the corporal.

'My God! Date, you idiot, name and address.'

Creon barked furiously: 'It's all there, man! It's written down! Let us get on with the business in hand.'

'Everything in its due course, Kyrios Creon. There is a certain procedure to be followed. I have my instruction.'

'Let me see it,' demanded Creon. He took the document to the window and read it interestedly. 'You're a damned fool,' he said at last. 'This has nothing to do with Kyrios Giorgios. He isn't English.'

'Well, how am I to know?' sighed the captain. 'All these people coming here, writers, artists, buying houses. How am I to know what they are? I don't understand it myself. Old ruins. Old rocks. Not even a cinema. Not even a wheeled vehicle. Do *you* like this place, Corporal Constantopolis?'

'No, Captain.'

'There you are. You must excuse us, Kyrios Creon. We weren't born here like you, and we're not artistic like the Kyrios. Are you artistic, Constantopolis?'

'No, Captain.'

'I suppose it's a different point of view,' the captain said tiredly. 'Are all those friends of yours going to buy houses too? That artist fellow who lives with his mother —?'

'It isn't his mother,' I said, giggling slightly. 'It's his wife.'

'Go on! There's no accounting for tastes. Mark you, the other one is a fine woman. The wife of that skinny writer. There's a woman for you. It's no wonder they haven't got a child between them when they're sorted out like that.' The captain cast a lewd eye at George. 'You're doing better, aren't you?'

'Creon!' George whispered tightly. 'I'm going *mad*!'

Creon blew his nose and adjusted his spectacles.

'Captain Gregorio! You're a damn' fool and you're wasting our valuable time. Have you any further business with the Kyrios?'

'Oh no,' said the captain. 'Except that his permit has been renewed. For one year, it says. What did you do with the permit, Constantopolis?'

'It's in your pocket, Captain.'

'Oh yes,' said the captain. 'I remember now, I put it there for safety. You don't think you could get me that tractor, do you, Kyrios?'

'I'll try,' George said weakly, and held out a shaking hand for the permit.

'And you tell that Irishman that his permit has come in too. For three months.'

Outside Katsikas' store Creon snorted to himself, 'They have nothing to do, that's the trouble with them.'

'All the same,' Sean said, 'it does make one rather uneasy. Any one of us might be thrown off the island at any minute.'

'Bah!' said Creon. 'Not while I am here. Do you think I have no influence? Eh? All the same, I had better see about having that man removed. He's a fool. I told him so.'

'Someone wrote EOKA on our steps last night,' Lola said. 'I was a bit hurt. I thought they liked us.'

'Ignore it!' Creon barked. 'Ignore it!'

Ursula smiled malevolently at Henry. 'Henry has a crowd of small boys following him all the time now. He buys them off with *drachmae*.'

'Oh, shush!' said Henry, and blushed.

Someone remarked mildly that all the EOKA business was likely to ruin Greece's growing tourist trade.

'Tourist trade? *Tourist* trade, madam! Do you think that there is a single Greek who would spare even a thought for *tourist* trade when he is fighting for freedom? Eh?'

I had never seen Creon so angry nor so Greek. I wondered suddenly if perhaps his association with us foreigners was becoming an embarrassment to him. I felt sad and guilty at the same time, but I could not put the thought away. Damn nationalism, I thought. Damn all flags, damn all slogans, damn passports and permits and visas and dossiers which arbitrarily label one Friend and another Enemy, one Black and one White, and without which one no longer has any legal right to exist at all. Damn my own naivete too in believing for a minute that one was going to dodge labels and categories even on this small grey rock in the Mediterranean. I thought of my son, who had stood up behind his desk at school in all the eight-year-olds agony of tears and conspicuousness to refute his teacher's assertion that the English were beasts and bloody butchers. I thought of my wild little daughter whooping through the lanes with her yellow hair flying, playing at revolutions. I thought of my baby, born a stranger in a strange land who would probably have to learn his mother tongue as a foreign language.

I thought of the safe anonymity of the office desk, the furnished flat, the monthly salary cheque, the insurance policy, the hot, stale smell of the herd and the will-less, witless way one had shambled along in the middle of it. It had seemed a glad thing to declare against all that; to declare for individuality, for risks instead of safety, for living instead of existing, for faith in one's own ability to build a good rich life from the raw materials of the man, the woman, the children, and the talents we could muster up between us. 'We will go and live in the sun,' we had said, and George had got up from his desk and walked out whistling.

Casting up accounts I came to the conclusion that we had done better than we had any right to expect. We had increased ourselves by one, we had provided a home for our little tribe; a contract just arrived from our publishers assured us that we had succeeded in guaranteeing ourselves food for the best part of the next year. With a bit of luck and enough hard work it even seemed possible that before long we might even be able to indulge ourselves in a few luxuries.

But would we be left alone to do it? Was there really any room in the world for people who did not fit neatly into the filing system? Perhaps one would be forced to take sides, declaring For or Against ... or perhaps one was going to be filed away without any choice at all.

7

As the sun strengthens and rides higher the whitewashed walls begin to take on a dazzle at noontime. The terraced houses shimmer among the prickly pears and aloes. At morning and evening the harbour front seems to slip and slide in a moving green-gold mesh of water reflections. All bare and innocent the island lies under the sun, or faintly, distractingly, luminous under the moon. The world smells of sea salt, herbs, springing flowers. Something is imminent, something wonderful, something lucky, I don't know what — perhaps the Death and Resurrection of Easter, for which the town is preparing joyfully.

Housewives are busy with whitewash pails and brushes tied to long poles, the donkeys all have nice new canvas bags tied under their backsides, on Saturday mornings the municipal cleaning hose shoots white jets across the pink cobbles of the quay, and in front of the Hotel Poseidon the marble admiral and his attendant lion ride triumphantly on leaping rainbow columns of water.

Now one hurries along behind the mail sacks to the post office, or loiters behind the pickets with the morning crowd to watch the *Sirina* come in and the rowing boats approaching. And though the mail produces nothing astonishing, and the rowing boats mostly deposit the usual quota of black shawls, trussed hens, potted shrubs, and weekending Athenians, occasionally a different face gazes out over the approaching mound of bodies and baggage, staring towards the shore with an expression that is becoming familiar in its mixture of anxiety, hope, and controlled desperation.

There begin to arrive the people who have dreamed of islands.

First the American pair who came at the same time as my baby. They are Toby and Katharine Nichols, both of them American by birth, European by education, and Greek by choice. At least, Toby is Greek by choice. Of Katharine I am not so sure, although her fine, intellectual face is kept innocent of make-up and her hair is braided neatly into two long plaits which hang down her back under a white scarf tied correctly in the old fashion of the island, still seen on very elderly women or occasionally on shepherds' wives who have not yet learned modern ways. She wears an apron over her modest print dresses and carries a basket wherever she goes, even to her daily Greek lesson at the house of the gymnasium teacher.

Toby has no need for Greek lessons. He speaks the language fluently, if rather nervously, and appears to be a little exasperated because Creon refuses to understand him and insists on speaking English. Toby's plump earnest face is mostly obscured by huge spectacles with thick tortoiseshell rims and an enormous

Greek-style moustache that has something of the same party disguise effect as Katharine's headscarves and aprons. Toby affects cheap fishermen's trousers and jerseys, shepherd's boots soled with old motor tyres, and carries an outsize *kombolloi* of amber beads.

They have rented the house of Little Cuckoo's cousin, in behind the waterfront, where they intend to stay for a year at least while Toby writes, we are told, a definitive work on mythology. Katharine, according to the same source, will devote her time to poetry. Little Cuckoo adds the information that they have paid their rent six months in advance, and that Tassos the carpenter is employed in fashioning a huge wooden bed platform such as is still used in the Aegean and was favoured by the peasants here until they learned about wire springs. Little Cuckoo is at a loss to understand it all. 'My cousin left her marriage-bed in the house for them. A very fine bed, with a new headpiece of silver metal.'

The cousin's house is a very large one, but the space is lost by a bad arrangement of many little rooms on different levels. Even now in April it is very hot and stuffy, particularly as Toby has hung all the walls and draped all the sofas with his collection of Greek rugs and donkeys' saddlebags. Katharine is adding to these from the selection brought to her daily by village women who are eagerly stripping their houses of all articles of home-woven merchandise. There is a rumour that even the nuns up at the convent are thudding away at their looms night and day to finish an outsize rug to cover the outsize bed platform.

Such faithful attention to the simple details proper to the simple life must be based on the solid plinth of an adequate private income.

When we went to tea with them Katharine, looking rather tense, was struggling with a recalcitrant charcoal fire that was smoking furiously under the white hood of the stove recess. Clouds of smoke billowed through the kitchen, the air stank of kerosene, and Katharine's fine, sensitive face was clownishly daubed with charcoal dust.

'Perhaps you would be good enough to show Katharine how to make a charcoal fire,' Toby asked with nervous deference. 'I am certain there *must* be a simpler way. She has been at it an hour and it still doesn't burn.'

'I'm sure I'll manage it, Toby dear,' Katharine said faintly, 'if I persevere just a little longer. I *know* it's only a matter of perseverance.'

It struck me as curious that behind the charcoal grate there stood a beautiful brand-new Buta gas cooking-range, a splendid thing of shining white enamel and scarlet taps that made me feel quite sick with envy.

'Have you run out of gas?' I asked sympathetically.

'Oh no.' Katharine poked ineffectually at a smoking mountain of paper and charcoal lumps. 'There's half a cylinder left yet. But Toby feels we must get the knack of living as *Greekly* as possible. If we're to fit in, you know. Toby feels that a gas range is a foreign intrusion, like an ice-box or something like that.' Her round blue eyes, streaming now in the smoke, glanced briefly at the nasty wire meat-safe hanging from the rafters. 'Toby thinks the gas range was a mistake,' she said flatly.

'My God!' said George, and looked wonderingly at Toby.

Toby was struggling to hook down a large bunch of dried mountain herbs from the kitchen rafters. 'When Kate has the fire going,' he said, 'I'd like you to try some of this. All the mountain people use it instead of tea, you know.'

'I know,' said George. 'They use it for constipation.'

'Oh no. Really?' Toby looked hurt. 'Then perhaps after all, Kate, we might just this time finish off what is left of the China.'

'Not *real* China tea?' we gasped.

'Oh yes,' said Toby. 'We have a little left. But by ourselves, you know, we always drink the herb tea.'

They declined an invitation to join the rest of the foreign population for dinner at Spiro's restaurant, not, I think, from any unfriendliness, but because they are truly afraid of a sort of contamination. Their conversion to the Simple Way is as narrow and as ardent as only an intellectual conversion can be. One has to respect their earnestness.

'Don't we live Greekly *enough*?' wondered Sean over Spiro's soiled tablecloth. And Lola, listening with open mouth to the description of the cooking-range, could only gasp:

'Mother of God! Gas taps *and* an oven! Would she let me use it to bake some pies?'

Come too is another American who has dreamed of islands. A tall, gangling fellow of thirty-five or so, with wiry black hair close-cropped in the American fashion, and uneasy doggy-brown eyes. He speaks of Back There with a sort of subdued horror. Apparently he has been drifting across Europe for many years, perhaps since the end of the war, hopelessly looking for himself in the sorrowful and anguished byways of foreign cities. He seems familiar with the most fashionable movements and the most fashionable vices. When he has been drinking he speaks the way Henry Miller writes: at other times his conversation is filled with literary quotations that one feels he has learned painfully in sad back rooms. But he wears his sophistication like borrowed clothes, uneasily, and his lost-dog eyes have a dreadful centre of purposelessness.

He is a painter, he says, but he hasn't been able to really get down to it in Europe. Here, in this simple clean place, without distractions, without temptations, he feels he will be able to work at last. He speaks so earnestly of this, and of Purpose and Art and Sincerity, that one wishes to believe it all as much as he does. But it seems as though he cannot begin work until his 'patron' sends him the money to buy paints, and in the meantime he sits around in the taverns getting drunk on credit and filling sketchbooks with demented abstracts concocted from spit and candle ends and a child's box of crayons.

Perhaps if he stays long enough the sun will work on him, the clear white light that reveals all things to be what they are rather than what one would wish them to be: one hopes that he might even find his sorry plumage of borrowed fashions to be unnecessary here, and dare to stand up in the simple nakedness of plain Sykes Horowitz. On an island, eventually, you are bound to meet yourself.

After Sykes came a White Russian, a bearded young man bearing as luggage a piece of pork and a case of blunt surgical instruments. His arrival has surprised no one more than Sean and Lola, since he has moved into their house and apparently intends to stay.

The house is owned by a mutual friend in Paris who lived here once for a year or so and perhaps dreams sometimes that he will do so again. In the meantime he lends his house to those of his friends who have reason to need an island. The young Russian's title to the use of it is equal with Sean's and Lola's, and he has suggested that they all live there together. Lola is willing, I think, particularly as the Russian has ordered a load of wood for the old pottery oven in the garden, and Lola has long wanted to dabble in ceramics. Sean is dubious, but since he finds the young man quiet, respectful, and well behaved, he hopes it might work out. In any case, I think he is too preoccupied to care. He has embarked on another novel and wants only to be left in peace to complete it. He is obsessed by the dual fact that he is now in his fortieth year and that the three novels he has written previously have not yet found a publisher: time is rushing past him — he is haunted by the spectre of a middle-aged schoolmaster who looks like himself but no longer dreams of islands.

The latest of the new arrivals has made everyone conscious of time. He came off the morning boat, a rather short young man with a beautiful brown throat and a sun-bright head. His feet were bare, and he wore only a pair of patched jeans, a rag of a scarlet shirt, and one gold earring.

Rather slowly and sleepily he shuffled along the quay, carrying a big artist's portfolio, a mule saddlebag in bright stripes and a tabby cat in a netted basket. Had he chosen to arrive in the faunskin of Dionysos, wearing an ivy crown, and carrying a fennel wand, the effect could hardly have been more electrifying.

'Do you think that young man is *real*?' asked Ursula, and Lola let out a whoop of absolute joy. 'Oh, wait, *wait*,' she said ecstatically, 'until Hippolyte sees this! He'll die of envy!'

''Ullo,' said the young man, stopping by our table and giving us the full treatment of a slow, white smile in a tawny young face. 'My name is Jacques. Can you tell me 'ow I go about finding a 'ouse 'ere?'

May

I

Christ is risen. The little lambs have been slaughtered, the fireworks exploded, the red eggs eaten, the tall, white candles burnt out, the paper lanterns put away. The flowery biers that bore Christ's bleeding body through moonlit lanes and along cliff paths by the sea are again relegated to upper church galleries to gather dust among cracked *ikons* and sacks containing very old skulls and thigh bones. Only Panyotis and Orestes, the village shoeblacks, are still drunk. They, with Tzimmy the pedlar — who is also drunk, but not more than usual — carried sacred banners in the Easter procession, like a trio of sly old mountain trolls rigged out incongruously in brocade and black satin skullcaps.

Redeemed, the islanders are heady with Grace and politics. Imminent minor elections have re-sparked the EOKA fervour and provided a new topic for arguments in coffee houses, barber shops, and on street corners.

Every Greek is a natural orator, and since an orator needs an audience any difference of opinion between two persons results inevitably in an appeal to bystanders: an accusation against or a claim for a certain political candidate can rock the whole waterfront with emotion. I watched with fascination an argument that began between two labourers unloading charcoal from a caique. Each put down his sack and appealed to God, to the lingering bit of sense left in the other's head, and finally to passers-by. Within two minutes a large crowd had gathered. The protagonists, their backs turned to each other, were each delivering an elaborated version of their argument to their section of the audience. Rapt, each in his own eloquence, they began to move in different directions, gesticulating, exhorting, appealing, declaiming. The crowd divided neatly into two sections and began to move also, each section drawing to itself further strength along the route taken. Finally, there was one huge milling mob around the steps of the post office, and another huge mob far, far away under the cannons on the fort. The waterfront was empty except for two abandoned charcoal sacks.

In all this nobody enjoys himself more than Creon. He is concentrated, curt; his lowered head and set shoulders look as forceful as a battering ram; in the taverns and coffee shops he is busy organising his hereditary block of voters, inherited along with the sponge business from his grandfather and father. It was instructive to watch him in action in Katsikas' Bar, where he was issuing instructions and directions to a group of shepherds — tall, straight-eyed old men who are each the patriarchs of clans that number up to thirty or forty souls, blood of their blood and flesh of their flesh.

None of these old men, direct descendants of the original shepherds who settled the island, can read or write (most of them, in fact, speak Albanian rather than Greek), but they listened with great dignity to Creon, and accepted a bundle of campaign posters to be pinned on trees or pasted on rocks around their hamlets.

George, glancing idly at one of the posters, was surprised to see that the face depicted there was that of the political candidate whom Creon had sworn to oust from office.

Had Creon changed allegiance? George asked.

'What! My dear George, the shepherds are not going to *vote* for this imbecile! But one of my agents has advised me that this idiot intends to play into my hands: he is actually coming to the island to try to canvass votes personally. So! I have merely told the shepherds that this is the picture of a man wanted by the police!' And Creon rubbed his hands together in satisfaction.

2

Here, in the house by the well, we launch ourselves into each day with the discipline and determination of a well-trained gun-crew who mean to blaze away as long as there is any ammunition left.

Day begins at dawn, when the baby wakes, and from dawn until the time when the bigger children are finally buttoned into their smocks and pelting off towards the precipitous flight of stone steps that soars up to the Down School, duties are strictly divided. By the time the school bell has clanged first warning I am already galloping off past St Constantine's with my market basket, while a tentative clicketing is issuing from the studio where George has set up the workbench and typewriter.

The studio is his action post for all the morning.

Even in its nakedness it is a lovely room, long and low-ceilinged, which because of its five arched windows seems to be mostly air. It hangs among tiled rooftops, soft now with orange moss and random grasses; among weed-grown lanes that appear, improbably, above the roofs, curling narrowly between high white garden walls; among grilled windows and bright brass hands quiescent on grey gates and doors, old balustraded balconies that hang crooked above tiled courtyards, high flat terraces; among lines of washing blowing, stiff moving bunches of citrus leaves sparked with minute scented blossoms, leaping vines scratching against crumbling walls, cascades of wistaria.

There is no sky in the five windows, but flights of neglected stone stairs leap up out of the lanes all about: from this strange room they might ascend to heaven. Mule trains descend, bearing mountain brushwood, water tanks, planks of pale new wood; two children climb up slowly, hand in hand, and turn on the stair to look into the room; our Mrs Silk appears, mumbling and prodding with her staff as she searches still for Sophia among the weeds exposed on a sunny wall. You feel that you have only to blink your eyes once and the hooves of the mules will be lifting delicately over the windowsill, and the children beside you, touching your hand.

The disadvantage of the room as a workroom is this very airiness. One had not realised — and I suppose one is deliberately blind to disadvantages when one wants something very much — that there were quite so many houses overlooking ours. Twenty windows round are private boxes filled with unabashed women and children, who jostle each other in their eagerness to see the curious spectacle of George seated at his typewriter. The terrace opening off the studio might as well be a public stage — and *there* go all my plans for nude sunbathing.

Nor had one realised quite how Up the Down School is. It rears above our tiled oriental roof so close that you can almost follow the lessons in progress, and during breaks the entire two hundred children line the iron railings, urging a very important Martin and Shane to shout messages down to us. If the neighbours' windows are the private boxes the school is the gallery, and the gallery is vociferous with enthusiasm. Perhaps Creon is right. Perhaps they will all get used to us in time.

But it is the baby who is the focus of the most intense interest and curiosity, perhaps because he is the first foreign child ever to be born on the island. Trying to keep a clinic routine here is to be Sisyphus, eternally rolling his stone uphill. The moment Booli lets out a roar of protest at being dumped down in his basket for his sleep, a neighbour materialises in the kitchen, which is *my* morning action post.

'The baby cries.'

'I hear it,' I say as politely as I can, without stopping from peeling the beans or fanning the charcoal fire or rinsing the diapers or sifting the lentils for pebbles. I cannot, in fact, afford to stop. Half an hour lost in the day means chaos at the end of it.

'But the baby *cries*.' The first gentle reproach has become real bewilderment.

'Never mind,' I say callously. 'It won't hurt him.'

The head of Kyria Heleni has intruded through the window. 'Excuse me, Kyria, I thought you might not hear. The baby cries.'

Little Aphrodite and Persephone patter in through the pink courtyard, hand in hand, piping urgently. 'The baby cries, Kyria. The baby *cries*!'

It would be nice to be able to wiggle my ears. 'What do you think these are?' I would say. 'Jug handles?'

But I continue with my kitchen duties with an outward show of calm, smile matter-of-factly at my visitors, and discourse briefly on the importance of a baby exercising its lungs, on the supreme importance of an early sound training in regular hours of sleeping and eating, on the preciousness of Routine. But inevitably, before I am halfway through my lecture, the ear-splitting shrieks of rage from the nursery have subsided into strangled gurgles through which can be heard that age-old maternal *lietmotif* of hissing, clucking, and gooing. Kyria Spirathoula's huge bottom appears in the trapdoor, and she backs carefully down the ladder into the kitchen, holding the small, bobbling bundle that is Booli, still purple with the last swallowed sob.

'I saw you had company, so I picked him up for you,' Kyria Spirathoula says blandly, looking me straight in the eye. 'I thought you might not have heard him crying.'

'Poor little baby ... koo-koo-koo-koo ... all alone up there ... it's cruel to leave him alone then, isn't it?' She is talking to the baby, of course, not to me. So are the other women, who are now passing him from hand to hand, jigging and bouncing and tweaking him, hissing and *poo-sou*-ing (a sort of formalised spit, repeated three times after any word of praise; that Evil Eye again). Booli is beginning to look frenzied. He opens his mouth and bellows.

'Ah, he is hungry then,' says Kyria Heleni sagely, and jolts him up and down more violently than ever, hissing like a guardian adder.

I say that he has just been fed.

'It's a touch of the sun,' says Kyria Spirathoula reproachfully, grabbing the baby from Kyria Heleni and jiggling in her turn. 'None of mine had a touch of the sun on their skins until they were walking.'

'He ought to have his hands tied down,' Little Cuckoo whispers. 'Waving about like that without any wrappings.'

I would like to say that at this stage I take the baby firmly and return him to his basket, where he falls to sleep immediately, thus vindicating modern methods of baby training. In fact, I do take him firmly and return him to his basket, and there he lies screaming all the morning, jiggled and hissed out of his senses, poor little thing. The ladies stand around the lane outside in dignified groups, whispering and nodding to each other and shaking their heads sadly.

'Why don't you tell the old faggots to mind their own bloody business!' George shouts down to me. He doesn't get any more sleep than I do — and he is trying desperately to meet a publication date.

'It's no use telling them to mind their own business,' I yell back in exasperation. 'The baby is their business. He's the whole damn' town's business! I'm trying to *educate* them!'

'Well, do you think you could do it more *quietly*? Or even just give in?'

I'm damned if I'll give in, even though the education programme seems to be working in reverse. I feed Shane with cunning propaganda to disseminate among the neighbouring houses. Shane returns with gruesome stories of babies who were allowed to go on crying *and died.*

'Mummy,' says Shane beguilingly, 'Kyria Spirathoula says she has an old sucker of little Yanni's that she isn't using now and she'll give it to us for Booli. You put sugar on it and it's *so* nice.'

Creon stormed in the other day, demanding to see his godson. It was clear from the blackness of his brow that tales of my unnatural behaviour towards my child had already drifted to his ears.

'Hmmph!' He grunted and changed his spectacles to peer into the basket where Booli, brown as a nutmeg, sprawled stark naked in the sun. And after a long surveillance, with the faintest intonation of surprise, 'There's nothing the matter with him, is there?'

Unfortunately, that same day the midwife just 'happened to be passing'. It had to be my luck that not only was the baby crying, but I was not even there. She had gone by the time I returned from the market, but Booli was bound up in blankets and pinned until he couldn't move a muscle, and George was looking at me in anxious embarrassment.

'Look, don't you think he *is* a bit thin for his age? I mean, do you think you ought to feed him a bit more? She said you ought to feed him every time he cries.'

Now they've got me into such a state that *I'm* worrying. And then Lola bounces into the kitchen and says brightly: 'What a *day*! Too lovely to work, isn't it? Sean and I are going to picnic on the other side of the island.'

There will never be a picnic for me, never again. This is only the early stage of wails and wind. But then there is the teething, and then the crawling, and then the toddling. There is a vista of lines full of diapers going on and on for ever. There are sterilising things and grating things and mashing things and straining things. There are mule kicks, mad dogs, precipitous stairs, harbour waters, diphtheria, cholera epidemics, and polio …

'Oh, *why* did we do it?' I wail in tiredness and sudden panic.

'There, love. He might be a Shakespeare, or a Rembrandt, or a Beethoven.'

To which I can only reply, 'Well, I'll never know, because by that time I'll be dead.'

And young Shakespeare, smelling richly of ammonia, baby powder, and regurgitated milk, belches loudly, slobbers a froth of bubbles, and slowly crosses his eyes.

3

It was very sadly that we stood on the waterfront and waved goodbye to Henry and Ursula: we had hoped that she might have won out for once.

'Creon, do keep on about a house for me, will you?' Her voice was pleading as she leaned over the stern of the caique to shake hands for the last time. Three mule loads of possessions were stacked on the deck — the expensive Linguaphone equipment, the special baggage, the camp stretcher for the back of the estate waggon with the inflatable mattress and the foam-rubber cushions — affirmations of Henry's faith in his own philosophy of always having the best, whether you can pay for it or not.

'Yes, Creon, a house with a great big cellar, don't forget, for that forge. Zoë, you keep at him. And write to us. And work well.' But his tousled head was already turning away to the sea, to the mainland across the water. From the moment he had stepped aboard the caique the island was behind Henry. In the months of winter ... in the light and the storms and the rocks and the sea ... in thistles, goats, and flowering thorn ... below the bean sacks in Katsikas' store and Spiro's advertisement for Fix Beer ... in all these things he had found an imperative direction post. But whether his way could lead him back nobody could know.

We stood and waved until the caique rounded the breakwater and we could no longer see the bright pink blob of Henry's eager face above his loud horsey jacket, or the angular figure of Ursula wound about the mast with one thin arm raised, Medea-like, in tragic farewell. 'Goodbye ...' we called through cupped hands, and 'Goodbye ... goodbye ...' drifted faintly back across the water.

A wistfulness fell on everybody. Now, in retrospect, those long months of difficulties, discomforts, boredom, and forced propinquity appeared singular for their richness of adventure, discovery, enthusiasm, comradeship. This fair and sunny island, glittering in its blue setting like a many-faceted jewel, was different from that island where we had waded through torrents, watched for a sail like castaways, seen great thunderstorms splitting the mountains with Homeric flashes, where we had been cold and discouraged and hungry or ablaze with the brightness of private visions, where in the pallid beam of a kerosene lantern we had talked whole nights away.

Now around the pink arc of the port the pretty painted boats rode easily — a children's carousel — and the market stalls were heaped with plenty. In front of Johnny Lulu's café three German girls, hefty pieces in trousers and straw hats, had set up three easels: earnestly, in cubes, they were recording Lotus Land.

Creon blew his nose loudly and said with a fair attempt at jauntiness, 'Ladies and gentlemen, shall we now adjourn to Katsikas' Bar?'

But Lola had to get home to watch the Russian boy, Feodor, firing the pottery oven. I had to rush through marketing and retrieve Booli from Kyria Spirathoula before he learnt too many bad habits.

George and Sean were already mentally on their ways back to their typewriters. Zoë had to find fish for her cats. And even Creon, I suspected, in spite of his conventional gallantry, had some crafty political business in hand which demanded his personal attention in Panyotis' coffee house.

Nobody really had time to waste sitting in a stuffy, dirty little grocer's shop.

4

If the island is no longer 'our' island, it is very lovely nonetheless. A summer island, a painter's paradise, just enough off the beaten track to be an authentic 'discovery', simple still, and strong with its own personality. 'Quite unspoilt,' people are heard to say. 'The essence of Greekness. An absolute gem.'

Toby and Katharine are still living as Greekly as all get out. Toby, who doesn't smoke, has acquired a cigarette lighter; one of the primitive models that have about three yards of red cord for a wick. He makes great play with this in the taverns where the sly old bums wink at each other and gather around him as around a horn of plenty. Sometimes, to be convivial, Toby smokes with them, puffing away in the middle of his huge moustache like a small boy bent on proving his manliness. But, alas, drink with them he cannot. To his mortification and bitter shame, *retzina* turns him up.

He is finding it difficult to begin on his vast work of scholarship. It is taking Katharine longer than he had expected to learn the Greek ways of housewifeliness: that charcoal fire still smokes obstinately, and she cannot quite get the hang of drawing water from the well. Besides, she needs constant help in her dealings with tradesmen and neighbours. And Toby has taken over her Greek lessons himself, as they both felt she was not making enough progress with her tutor.

'And what about your poetry, Katharine?'

'*Poetry!*' says Katharine, in a faint expiring voice.

The villagers like them both very much, finding them anxious to be friendly, easy to cheat, and ever so slightly *tralós*, that is to say, dotty.

But the real source of village entertainment is the young man Jacques, who has rented a tiny white house on the cliff-top where he lives alone, very French, with only his cat for company.

Cassandra, the girl who does our washing, has an Aunt Theodora whose house overhangs Jacques' terrace, and Aunt Theodora says that the cat is pregnant. She seems vaguely shocked by this.

Aunt Theodora, via Cassandra, is also our medium for the information that Jacques pays one hundred and fifty *drachmae* a month for his two-roomed, unfurnished house, that he borrowed a bucket and a whitewash brush from his landlady on the day he moved in, and that he can be seen every morning squatting on the terrace under the vine with his cat, sharing raw eggs, which they both eat by sucking the egg through a hole in the shell.

The neighbouring ladies are agog and the young girls wildly giggly at the spectacle of him doing his washing regularly by the communal well. Cassandra says there is a line rigged up on the terrace that is hung twice a week with an orderly array of patched jeans and shirts and the brilliant handkerchiefs that Jacques wears knotted apache fashion around his brown throat. Cassandra, who is a sensible, phlegmatic girl, is rather impressed by such novel domesticity in a male: her shining eyes and hushed voice betray the fact that even she has been touched by the general contagion of excitement.

Gossip and scandal collect about him. He has been seen at the window — this Aunt Theodora swears — wearing nothing but one of his scarves tied as a G-string. It is rumoured that he sleeps on goatskin mats. Aunt Theodora has seen him shaking them over the terrace, and she knows for a fact that there is no furniture in the house other than an old phonograph, very wheezy and temperamental. Apparently there is only one record too, a silly, popular *bouzouki* song called 'Par Epano', which can be heard twangling down the cliff side, over and over, all day long.

Neighbouring ladies who for some unexplained reason have had business near the house very late at night have testified to whispering and soft laughter intermingled with 'Par Epano'. But here I feel that their ears might be listening to their imaginations, since the village girls are notoriously moral (I have heard enough of the frustrations of other foreign young men to be reasonably certain of this), and at the moment there are no other eligible women except the three German girls, who appear to be wholly occupied working out perspectives with Pepsin, Strepsin, and Amylopsin.

However, the strict morality of the village girls does not prevent them from choosing the path that passes Jacques' house, and to linger under his terrace while they extract pebbles from their shoes and giggle nervously. Sometimes, standing at the window with the cat in his arms, he looks down lazily at the girls and his eyelids droop and he fingers the tiny gold hoop glinting at his ear against the coarse fair spikes of his hair.

Lola, who has entertained him at luncheon, says he is quite a pleasant young man, and she suspects that he sleeps on a bed, just like other people. I think that's carping. If he doesn't sleep on a goatskin he ought to.

'Did he eat raw eggs for lunch?' I asked.

'He did not,' said Sean. 'He ate a very good *tarama salata*, stuffed kalamaria, and the best part of a lemon meringue pie. The lunch,' he added with gloomy relish, 'took Lola the best part of two days to prepare.'

'You try making a lemon meringue pie without an oven!' said Lola. Now, in these days of warmth and plenty, Lola has come into her own. She blooms in the sun. Her olive skin shines. Unrestrained by corsets, or girdles, and nourished on an unavoidable diet of starches, her flesh romps and billows in huge, shivery waves that burst over bodices growing tighter and tighter: on little light feet, incongruously shod in those clumsy shepherd's boots, she moves to the sound of ripping seams and popping fasteners, cursing automatically as she fumbles in her shopping basket for another safety-pin.

'Think,' says Hippolyte, entranced, 'how splendid — nude — with a cornucopia of *apples*!' Inevitably, Hippolyte adores her. She is so large, so generous, so ready to laugh and to gossip, and so completely unshockable. To Hippolyte she is like a cosy, unexpected hearth at which even he, an outcast, can put down his burden of shame and guilt and warm his empty hands and his poor, empty heart. This is Lola's gift — and her danger. Her home is open to anyone who cares for food and wine and talk. Hippolyte, the Swedes, Jacques, tall Sykes Horowitz (still loping to and from the post office with an air of quiet desperation and a volume of Rilke's poetry), even lately the three German girls — all find it easy to 'drop in on Lola' for cups of coffee and wine and meals.

Making meals is her joy. She shops along the quay dramatically, in a series of pounces and swoops that are accompanied by cries of rage or despair or triumph. Nicko is charging a *drachma* more for coffee! 'Thieving bastard!' screams Lola into Nicko's smiling face. Pantales has sold all his artichokes and there is no caique until tomorrow. The dandyish butcher Apostoli is mincing along from the direction of the slaughterhouse with a gardenia in his teeth and — joy! — the naked, bloody carcase of a real pig slung about his crimson shoulders!

On the spot, menus are made, discarded, improvised; there are appeals, rejections, hagglings, denunciations — there is not a shopkeeper in the village who does not respect Lola with his whole heart. So she surges along, with Sean following after in his gentle, sorrowful way, wincing a little at her more dramatic excesses, but dutifully carrying the rapidly filling baskets, and accepting with resignation the backlash of her shopping exasperations.

Lately it has been Feodor who has been carrying the baskets. 'He might as well be useful, and it keeps him out of Sean's way.' A bearded, goaty figure, he shambles along behind Lola like a tired satyr, occasionally exploding with a honk of laughter as if at his own degradation, or absent-mindedly scratching his bottom with a clay-coated hand. Across a bouquet of crisp curled lettuces and pungent spring onions I encounter his little dull, wet hopeless eyes and am secretly appalled.

'Lola, how can you *bear* him?'

'Well,' says Lola, 'he isn't really so bad, and the point is that the poor wretch hasn't any money. We can't really toss him out, since he has as much claim to the house as we have, and if we move ourselves I don't know how he's going to eat. He's very polite, you know, and he keeps himself busy with his potting.'

'What is it like?'

'Mud-coloured,' says Lola on a sudden whoop of good humour. 'Phallic. And invariably cracked.' Her expansive flesh is quivering with laughter. 'Sometimes I think of Feodor down at the kiln making mud-coloured jugs, and me up in the studio making mud-coloured paintings, and Sean locked in his room writing mud-coloured prose, and I wonder why on earth we all don't simply stop and go and sit in the sun.'

Meanwhile Sean grows peaky and tired-looking and there are blue marks like bruises under his eyes. He seldom talks about his writing. He is working hard. And worrying hard.

'Take it more easily,' George tells him. 'You've the time and the chance and the talent. That's all you need. You'll write a fine novel.'

'Ah yes?' says Sean, with one of his little derisive grins. 'I've been looking through my collection of little printed slips lately, and I said to myself … suppose the buggers are right? Suppose,' and his grin stretched bleakly, 'I'm no damn' good?'

5

A fig-tree marks the point where the cliff path turns and plummets down towards the sea. Then, at the bottom of the path, there are twenty descending stairs, three rock platforms cemented over to make sunbathing levels, an arching cave roof with a jagged hole where the green light slips and slides mysteriously in the sea-smelling purple, an iron ladder for the timorous, and a long, low rock crooked slightly, like a scaly finger around the deep-plunging shelf where we swim.

All down the gulf the islands and islets rise in radiant humps and spires — knuckles and fingertips reaching up from legendary drowned lands. Old things lie under this glass green skin of sea, scaled things, slimed things, crusted things, still potent in the imagination. Who knows what scuttles silently across this sea floor, or what might one day stir and shake itself and rise, all barnacled and dripping salty weeds?

I thought today how beautiful my children have become in this deeply natural world, thin, brown, hard creatures, still unconscious of their own grace or even of the extravagance of beauty in which they move and have their being: for them it is no more to be observed than the number of times their sharp little breasts rise and fall breathing it in.

The sun streamed heat over the shelf where we lay watching them, their arrow-straight naked bodies hurtling from the cave lip thirty feet down into the water. The sea was so much like glass that the explosive jets of their impacts were somehow surprising, as though one had expected the surface to shiver and splinter into fragments instead. Through the churn we could see them wavering down and down along the spiny shelf and curving up again to the air and the sun — the thin scrawl of Martin's legs threshing, the slowly closing fan of Shane's glinting hair. They broke the surface pearled and gasping, and scrambled out on the rocks to climb up to the cave roof and leap again and again.

Sprawled inert under the great warm melting waves of light, I was glad that we had chosen to live in the sun. To live in the sun is reassuring. All is open, all revealed. Here are no deceptions, but the bare truth of things. I think that no beauty has ever been as true for me as this beauty of rocks and sea and the beauty of mountains that rush up between the blue and the blue, skirted only with austere white terraces of houses simplified to the purest geometry of planes and angles. It seems to me that we have become simplified too, living here, as though the sun has seared off the woolly fuzz of our separate confusions: the half-desires irresolutely sought, the half-fears never more than half vanquished, the partial attainments half-rejected in perplexed dissatisfaction. Shedding so much we are stripped to our bare selves, lighter, freer, and impoverished of nothing but a few ridiculous little self-importances.

Through the hot stillness sounds come distinctly — a splash of oars, the sharp yelp of the dog Max protesting against a bath, the children's voices calling away away, and from the village the clear, bright sound of a single bell. A passing bell again. In these last few weeks the passing bell has rung often. The old people die in the resurrection of the year, the old grey women and the old brown men who whiffled and snickered on their doorsteps waiting for the sun to come again; not a church doorway that has not revealed the black box, the sharp, aged profile pointed to the ceiling and clay-coloured against a formal frieze of grieving women.

Here the dead are not hidden away, but carried through the lanes in open coffins for everyone to see. Turned up to the sun the mute, ancient faces go jolting by, exposed for the last time to this clear white light that reveals death as impersonally as it reveals life. Looking down into the dead face of an old grandmother one is reminded that time incises deeply, cruelly, ineradicably, that decay is inherent in all living things. See, it is death, nothing more — an event in life — as significant or unsignificant as being born.

But how good it was to be alive and sprawled in the sun; how fine and free to dive from the highest rock above the cave-lip, willing one's spread arms to hold one arched in air. It was a day to attempt the unreasonable, so close it seemed, so almost within one's power to defy the laws of gravity. Launched in an arc above the waiting sea it seemed possible that one might hang there for a moment before the downward plunge ... or even soar on, on and on like a bird soaring across the brilliant gulf.

'What's the damage, Icarus?' George asked mildly, helping me out. But the damage proved slight for the joy of the aspiration — a grazed shin scraped on the ledge that plummets down below the cave, and a foot full of sea-urchin spines.

We came home salty, tangled, with the sun lying warm under our skins, to find the washing finished, the stone floors cool and clean from Cassandra's scrubbing, and the baby asleep in his basket under the lemon tree with Cassandra sitting beside it mending the sheets.

'Look,' said Cassandra, 'your vine has little bunches of grapes already. And the plums are ripening. It is almost summer.'

Signs of Summer

An old man in a braided jacket, white fustanella like a ballet skirt, long white stockings and turned-up red shoes with pom-poms on the toes.

He leans on a crooked staff and ambles slowly up and down the waterfront, burping and mumbling and mashing his gums in some private querulous soliloquy as he hitches his skirt or tweaks at the tassels on his jacket. The costume obviously is hideously uncomfortable; he has to walk with his legs wide apart to allow for the yards of stiff ruching that pass between them.

'Look, Kate, this is the real thing! Isn't he absolutely marvellous?' Toby Nichols is charmed and offers the old man to Katharine like a compensation for the charcoal fire and the outdoor privy. Even Katharine lights up momentarily. Because the old scoundrel certainly does look the real thing, and will make himself a steady little income all through summer by looking the real thing whenever a tourist's camera or an artist's easel is in sight. But he is querulous about it, and responds snappishly to the raw badinage of Orestes and Panyotis, for he is getting very old and dressing-up really is a lot of trouble. His daughter-in-law is furious if he spills anything on his skirt, for it takes two days to wash and iron …

Socrates' hat. A wide sombrero of plaited straw, beneath which Socrates' little round Turkish face beams like a battered lantern. He has lately sold two houses to wealthy Athenians, a German doctor has arrived with the intention of buying a summer villa, soon there will be boatloads of tourists looking for accommodation, and besides — Socrates is in love. Aunt Electra is so angry she has not made his favourite beans-and-onion stew for a month. 'Let him go to *her* for beans-and-onion stew,' Aunt Electra mutters. 'See how he'll get on. *She's* too fine to dirty her hands with cooking!' And Aunt Electra sets her mouth in a thin tight line and tosses her gross grey head like an arrogant girl, but bursts into jealous tears at last. For it is a bitter thing to her to have loved and spoiled her little Turkish foundling for nigh on forty years, and kept him free from impure thoughts, only to be threatened with a chit of a daughter-in-law at a time when she might fairly consider herself to be safe at last.

'He's bald!' she weeps angrily. 'His belly is like a pot! He has rheumatics! What does he want with a wife at his time of age?' So she deprives him of beans-and-onion stew, and Socrates trots on his way singing, not even noticing, committing the final outrage of clipping the first gardenia from Aunt Electra's potted bush and carrying it to Maria. And Maria, who is a kind, twinkling sort of girl, accepts the gardenia gravely, and waits until she is inside her shop before her mirth engulfs her ...

Maria's shop. Made over to her properly by deed at the notary public's office in the monastery by her father, old Stamatis, who has had the shop for fifty years, like his father before him. Sponges they sold, and nails and screws and hooks and fishing lines, earthen cooking pots, tinware and ironware, ships' lanterns, dead-eyes, strings of cork, and lead sinkers.

But Maria now has fixed up the front of the shop with glass showcases from Athens and rows of shelves on which she has arranged copper pots and bowls, shell necklaces, peasant embroideries, bead bags, cute belts made from rope and painted ship's tackle, straw donkeys, sponge purses, fishermen's caps and jerseys, rope-soled sandals, Mykonos shirts, model windmills, and the rest of the gay trivia the tourists love.

At the back of the shop old Stamatis still potters about stubbornly, carefully smoothing out his cement mould and twisting little paper spills to receive the molten lead he is boiling up in a tin coffeepot over a charcoal fire.

'I'm making sinkers. *Sinkers.* Made them every year since I was a boy. Don't know what that girl of mine is up to. She'll ruin us all with her nonsense. People aren't going to buy *that* rubbish.' And he glances wistfully at a life-size waxen dummy with mutton-chop whiskers, dressed in the fashion of fifty years ago, who smirks back at him from the old crates of nails and hooks and festoons of wooden dead-eyes and ships' shackles.

'That's all right,' says Maria shrewdly. 'But Father's old now and doesn't see that times have changed. This island is coming on. Athenians are buying houses. There are more tourists every year.'

'Tourists?' Creon glares at Maria and jabs briefly with his finger in the direction of the street. Jacques is shuffling slowly past, barefooted, a battered Florentine straw hat tipped over his eyes, and a torn pink shirt unbuttoned to the waist and tied casually in a knot. (One cannot fail to notice that he crosses the width of the quay to pass by the easels of the three German girls, nor that the youngest of them, the one with the heavy braids of hair, looks up from her painting with her mouth open and a brighter colour than usual staining her plump cheeks.)

'Tourists?' Creon snorts dismissively. 'Bums and perverts, my girl! Bums and perverts! There's not a moral nor a penny piece among the lot of them! The island is finished, young woman, and don't let that fool Socrates tell you otherwise. All the same, since you have committed yourself to this folly, you had better give me your account books to look after. A woman can't keep accounts.'

The boats. In sheds and basements, in lanes and doorways, there are little boats lying upside down or on their sides in every state of repair. There are splintered oars, lengths of new pine planking, peeled sticks, pots of paint, and a smell of hot pitch and petrol. A jet of blue flame illuminates the machine shop where engines are being repaired, in each of the boat-building cellars a pale curved skeleton of ribs and templates is slowly taking shape, and under the cliff by the slaughterhouse a gnome with an adze lovingly shapes a slim, straight tree trunk into a mast. Even the small children are fashioning boats from bits of tin and pieces of wood. One can smell the long days coming, the long blue days to sail, to row, to drift, to fish, to make excursions along the cliffs and to the islands of the gulf.

On the way to the *agora* I come upon George squatting beside an upturned hull and a can of hot tar. A wrinkled ancient stands by with a tolerant smile, watching George caulk seams. On George's face is an expression of infinite love.

'When the royalties come in,' he says, 'we'll buy a boat of our own.' But he spits three times carefully and crosses his fingers.

6

Despite Creon's warnings of 'the grippe', we are swimming every day. One's mouth has a permanent salty taste, one's skin is all prickles and goose-shivers as the first fiery coat of sunburn settles into a pale but authentic tan that defines the brief white triangles left by bathing suits. I regret the whiteness of the triangles, and those windows overlooking our terrace — even the briefest bathing slip seems immodest in the sun.

'May you wear it with health!' says Archonda the sempstress politely as she hands over two scraps of pink cotton which she has machine-stitched to my directions, and then she giggles wildly. Archonda thinks we are as mad as hatters.

In the afternoons now there are often other swimmers at the cave. Sleek, wet heads bob idly past on the sun-dazzle; the rock ledges are spread with near-nude bodies that are sprawled inert like limp starfish.

One learns to recognise people anew. The German girls are not easels and khaki trousers after all, but great marbly limbs and round maiden breasts, unexpectedly beautiful in a large sculptural way even in dowdy woollen suits of maroon, purple and rusty black. Sean is pink and bony, with sharp shoulderblades unfolded like wings and tender pink feet that are awkward on the spiky rocks. Sykes Horowitz, whom one had thought to be thin, has a flabby little belly and a big, flattish rump, mournful somehow. And then the milk-white Swedes, looking terribly vulnerable without their clothes — northerners who cannot lie easily under this great glowing sun but must *occupy* themselves with throwing a ball about, splashing noisily, or earnestly making collections of various forms of sea life for discussion and classification.

Only Lola is expectable, already nearly black and spilling out everywhere from a checked gingham arrangement she has made herself and not quite finished. And Jacques perhaps, who is tawny-gold and sleepy as a tomcat in the sun, stark naked except for a cunningly knotted handkerchief, the gold earring, and a caper flower that he twirls slowly between his beautiful teeth. He is scarred like a tomcat too — with a long cobbled mark that grooves the rippling triangle of his back like a bit of bad white darning.

'How did you come by that, Jacques?' Lola asked curiously.

Jacques' mouth curved sleepily, spilling a delicate cup of white petals and purple fringes against his flat brown cheek.

'I'ad to jump once,' he said, 'from a seventh-floor window.'

Hippolyte says that even if he believed in a God he would never forgive Him for showing such monstrous partiality.

'And it isn't as though Jacques *cares*,' he groaned, watching the dark gold body flip lazily into the sea. 'He goes about jumping out of windows! If I had a body like that I'd be terrified to take it across the street. Lola darling, will you just get at the small of my back with this damn' lotion? And across my chest where I plucked the hairs out. Gently, dear. It is excruciatingly painful.' Through shell-rimmed sunglasses he gazed pensively down to the water where Jacques lay floating with closed eyes, the caper flower still in his mouth and a damp forest of little golden tendrils glittering on his breast and belly. 'Or perhaps I'll let it grow properly. In *spit* curls. Oh, it's wicked,' Hippolyte sighed, 'that he can paint too.'

'So can you,' said Lola soothingly, dabbing gently with the lotion. 'At least, you can if you'd only bother to work.'

'But what am I working *for*?' Hippolyte cried violently. 'I don't believe in anything I do! I don't believe in myself! I don't believe in anything at all! And my hair is falling out *in handfuls*!'

In his cry there was a note of real tragedy that I recognised with a pang of sympathy, remembering the crowded buses lurching through the monstrous gloom of the darkest day that ever was, and myself sobbing uncontrollably at the end of the Tottenham Court Road queue because my fingernails were soft and tearing on the mesh of my shopping-bag. One's fingernails are tearing off, one's hair is falling out in handfuls, a tooth is loose, there is a new line, a grey hair ... one's youth is passing, is past, and one is still at the end of the queue, waiting for buses that scream past already overcrowded and bound for uncertain destinations.

Here, spread starwise on the shining cliffs above the shining sea, these seem treasonable thoughts. The warm rock is actual, the long-legged ant exploring a drop of spilt suntan lotion, the gull wheeling a confident white arc above the shimmering islets, the brown children tumbling in the water, the baby whiffling uncomprehendingly under its improvised awning.

On the ledge below, Jacques, all wet and shining like a seal, is persuading the youngest of the monolithic German frauleins to leave her companions and go gathering limpets in the cave with him, and it is a very pretty thing to see with what grace and practised skill he droops his eyelids a little to engage her half-frightened glance, and how his mouth quirks slightly in triumph as he holds her eyes fixed wide on his while he leans across and lightly tucks the caper flower in her long wet braid of hair. And she will go gathering limpets, of course, though the other girls are furious and cold towards her, and the Swedes look crestfallen in a vaguely baffled way, and Lola's swarthy flesh jellies with laughter as she buries her head in her arms. Everything, you would say, is as it should be under the sun. Ant, gull, child, man, woman, is each fulfilling the imperative of its being.

Yet looking at the wet heads bobbing and the naked limbs lolling one cannot but reflect with Hippolyte that what Nature gives she gives with monstrous partiality, strewing inequalities of time, place, sex, heredity, inclinations, manners, customs, with an irresponsibility that is breathtaking. She makes one a man who had far better have been a woman, she brings another into a materialistic society that has no room for him, one inherits a weak chest, one a tendency to fat, one a culture that sickens him and for which another, born without traditions, will long for as for a birthright.

It is a diverse and tantalising collection of human beings sprawled about these rocks and ledges on a hot cliff far from their native lands, insurgents all who have rebelled against the station in which it pleased God to place them. What devious roads brought them to this small island, what decisions and indecisions, what driftings, what moments of desperation and hope? And what are they looking for? What do they expect to find here, an Australian journalist, an Irish schoolmaster, an American misfit, an exotic outrider from the St-Germain-des-Pres?

A breathing space to try to redirect my life in a way of my own choosing, Sean might say perhaps. And Sykes Horowitz, laying his throbbing hangover on the open pages of Rilke, would almost certainly say something literary about the mystic pleasures of renunciation or Art and Sincerity, meaning Let me feel whole! For Jacques, sunshine, easy living, cheap wine, the pleasure of being simple in a very sophisticated way. And girls, of course. The gay and empty journey.

'Who, *me*?' Hippolyte giggles, feeling good humoured again. 'Well, really, darling. I mean, this is a seamen's island after all. What do you *think* I expected to find here?'

An uninsurgent fly buzzes close at my ear. Dark against the glittering sky the children come, bringing sea treasures. George is already gathering up the towels and clothes. From a hundred churches the bells are ringing *espéres*. For even in revolt we are a whole Society in ourselves, bound to inexorable order and rhythm, circumscribed by laws and family conventions. For us there is the unquestioning way of shopping for supper, feeding the baby, getting the children to bed, and seeing Dinos about the drains.

June

I

Summer is in. Every day the sky seems higher, flatter, paler. The mountains have already lost their soft fuzz of spring green and at noon they glitter as if plated with bronze. On the cliffs the stone houses melt back into the rock and the white houses shimmer with an intolerable white brightness. The flowers are seared off the hills; the only vegetation now is spikes and thorns.

Outside our windows the women come early to the well; often I hear them chattering before Booli lets go with his first hungry wail of the day. Shrill, shrill the morning voices of the women above the lovely hollow clank and gurgle that is well music. Already they are agitated, querulous, quick to give way to exasperation — menless women who come to the well in their thick nightgowns and slippers and with their hair unbraided, for there is no one to see them. The howls and shrieks of their children, bird-early risers also, punctuate the gabble of gossip, the spurts of laughter, the quarrels.

My own children are clattering about in the bathroom and the kitchen or finishing off neglected homework. Sitting by the window feeding the baby I can hear the rhythmic oiled thud-thud-thud of the pump handle and high above my head the heavy jets of water clanging into the tank. George pumps water every morning for fifteen minutes, stripped to the waist — I suspect so that he can better admire his developing shoulder muscles in the small mirror that hangs on the wall facing the pump.

As early as this the heat is gathering. All warm my skin and warm my hair and warm the soft, heavy bundle of baby in my lap. The highest houses are leaping in a sudden vehemence of white, but on the lower slopes they are still pearly, soft, all heaped together like big blocks of marshmallow not quite set. The lane below me is running opalescence.

Wading through it comes Elia the water carrier leading his bony mule. Two cans of drinking water from the Sweet Wells at the head of the gorge for us, one for Kyria Spirathoula, and one for Kyria Heleni. Elia has a hibiscus flower stuck in the band of his panama hat.

Every morning he learns two words of English from George while he pours the drinking water into the huge ribbed stone jar in the kitchen. How much of the morning activity here, one suddenly realises, is concerned with water, this precious element that is valued at its worth, that is discussed for its sweetness, its coldness, its quality, that is fit welcome for a guest — presented in a shining glass centred neatly on a flower-bordered tray. Even the iceboxes have water tanks built in.

George and Elia are still bellowing cheerfully at each other in the kitchen when, further up the lane, Friday opens her gate and stands blinking at the morning for a moment before arranging herself on the doorstep with her embroidery basket beside her.

Friday is a dark, vigorous-looking young woman of twenty-four or so. Like the other women she wears her nightgown in the morning hours, but Friday's nightgown has a lace frill at the neck, and Friday's thick black hair is tied back with a ribbon. She lives with her sister Kyria Spirathoula and divides her waking hours between writing letters to lonely sailors who have advertised for penfriends and embroidering a trousseau for the marriage that must one day eventuate from the letters. Innumerable the tablecloths, the cushions, the teatowels, firescreens, doilies, chair-covers, mats, runners, and guesttowels already folded carefully away in the old seamen's chest in Friday's bedroom. Astronomical the number of minute stitches with which they are decorated — the ladies in crinolines and ladies in pokebonnets, the playing cards and Scotch terriers, the shepherdesses with sheep, the snow mountains and rustic bridges, the seahorses and dolphins. Friday is far too modern to use the traditional old island patterns, which are abstract and exquisite: Friday's motifs come from the pages of the genteel ladies' magazines.

She sings as she works, a harsh, high, plaintive song, indescribably angry. 'With a carnation at his ear and cunning in his eye, with a pocket always empty and a heart always full ... come for a walk with me, gypsy man'... I feel like an eavesdropper, listening to it.

Oh where is the lean gypsy man with the nonchalant carnation? When will Mr Right come striding up the lane to the triumphant concertina music of his creased sailor trousers, with the sun striking fire on his pointed, polished shoes and his bursting crimson heart suspended by a sequined ribbon from a posy of gardenias — for Friday, for graceful, accomplished Friday, that pure, lovely girl sitting in her doorway wearing out her little white fingers on endless pink shepherdesses? Where is Mr Right? Or Mr Halfway-right? Or even ... but this is only in the warm summer evenings, when the moon silvers the well and the scent of Kyria Heleni's jasmine nearly bowls you over, and Friday lays her embroidery aside and runs round and round the well screaming hysterically as she plays tag with the children in her nightgown with the lace frill at the neck ... where is Mr Wrong? Mr Anyone-at-all?

After supper, Friday and her friends make a formal promenade around the arc of the port, from the museum, past the shops and stalls and restaurants, as far as the cannons above the cave and then back again. The girls walk in twos and threes and fours, tenderly linked with soft arms clasped around each flowery waist, and each cascade of shining hair caught with a white ribbon or a gilt butterfly. The gymnasium boys are out promenading too, but walking very slow and lordly, swinging their key chains and *kombollois*, each with a Cyprus badge in his lapel and his gold-braided cap set straight above his eyes: only occasionally do they goose each other or deftly hook a foot across so that the next one goes sprawling.

All the more mature citizens are parading in groups, family groups almost as formal as the photographs on their walls. The matrons wear coats and skirts and high heels and carry patent leather purses which they clasp against their comfortable stomachs. The children are clean and well dressed and the little girls have huge starched bows perched on their heads. There is a purpose to this evening promenade, of course, apart from the pleasure of idly strolling through the mild and pleasant air in one's best clothes. The families with adult or maturing sons have their eyes on the girls. The mothers of daughters are watching the young men. This is the inspection paddock.

The girls are worth watching, but it is enough to break a mother's heart that the crop of young men is so scanty. Apart from a couple of wharf labourers still unwed and a few young tradesmen and fishermen — there is none of marriageable age worth a second glance from the respectable bourgeoisie — the pickings are slim indeed, for all the young men with any gumption have hooked off years ago and gone to sea.

The girls' flowery dresses and the matrons' coats and skirts and shiny purses and even the butterfly bows bobbing on the little sisters' crimped heads are provided by the monthly cheques sent back to the island from Greek merchant ships in far foreign places. Living is not expensive here, and whole families — including those intricate Grecian ramifications of grandmothers and aunts and in-laws and cousins of first and second remove — can live quite comfortably on one sailor boy. With a total island population of slightly fewer than three thousand, and four hundred of the adult males absent with the Greek mercantile marine, the economy of the island is entirely based on this. But while it is very comfortable, what are the girls to do for husbands? Many a mother must uneasily consider the possibility that there might also be other evening promenades in other lands — those mysterious lands that to her are no more than queer stamps on foreign envelopes … and dear Mother of God who knows how far those slant-eyed, dark-skinned girls might go to entice an innocent Greek boy …

The odds are long against the girls, but summer shortens them a little. For there is always the romantic chance that some wealthy Athenian, holidaying on the island, may surfeit of the brazen charms of the bare-legged, painted hussies who are unloading from the *Sirina* every weekend now, and recognise the true gold that shines in the pretty, modest face of an island girl. It's a long shot, but worth another new flowery dress, this time cut just a shade lower at the bosom.

2

Several of the great houses have already been opened up for the summer. The aristocrats are in their rightful places, high, high on the soaring cliffs, where for a few months they will be able to forget the concrete monstrosities clanging up in Athens and the big American automobiles and the shiny chromium bars where the new rich congregate.

Here nothing is changed: the Venetian chest, the pierced panels that enclose the winter bed-cupboard, the dull smoulder of gold caught in the light that burns always before the *ikon* box, the silk-smooth flagstones in the hall. Here in the tiled courtyard the geraniums still spill their acrid blood-red flowers from stained stone urns, the willow-pattern plates hang eternally on the whitewashed wall, the polished flintlock at the turn of the stair. Snippets and waste from old ancestral leavings.

On terraces as big as state ballrooms you may drink tea at five o'clock in an atmosphere so still and unhurried that even the tea itself has a timeless flavour — brought in a clipper ship, you suspect, stored in a carved chest, measured out in catties. Your hosts are gentle, cultured, gracious people, Englishly English or Frenchly French at will, with nothing in their easy manners or perfect accents even to remotely connect them with the fiercely whiskered gentleman in the exotic tasselled cap blazing away with a brace of pistols and glaring grimly from the gunsmoke-and-brimstone background set within the rich gold frame above the dining-room table … the fierce old feudal lord, the Turk fighter, whose flowing hair and formidable countenance is reproduced on every schoolroom wall in Greece.

See, this was the writing table he used, just as he left it. And here is his pistol, his telescope, a contemporary lithograph of his ship in action against the Turks, the battered log book with the thin brown spidery writing. And it is his ship's bell that rings as you enter the courtyard. Of course you may bring your friends to see the house.

Last summer we had three hundred visitors. There are so few of the old houses left in such a perfect state of preservation, with all the furniture of the period intact. So many of the older island families had to sell things, you know, in order to keep going.

Ironically, the *things* that the old families were forced to sell are coming back to the island gradually — Venetian chest, ladderback chair, carved sofa, willow-pattern plate and all. At least four houses have been sold in the last year to wealthy Athenians and are now being restored ... Genuine! Why, there isn't a lamp or a spoon in them that isn't in character, except perhaps for the luxurious tiled bathroom and the hot-water service run on Buta gas and the amusing bar-barbeque converted from the old bakehouse.

Look, here's that familiar writing desk again, and the model brig, and the telescope, and the painting of the tall-sparred ships locked in the smoke of Navarino. And surely that exotic whiskered gentleman in the gold frame ... surely it is The Hero?

'Why certainly, my dear,' says the lady with the long cigarette holder and the applied eyelashes. 'Didn't you know that he is a sort of ancestor of mine? Through a second-cousin, on my grandmother's side.'

'Next you will come and visit *my* house,' a stout, blonde woman invites us with some complacency. 'I have *many* things of a genuine character, and of most things I have *two*.' She smiles a secret smile of satisfaction and folds her beringed hands over a high, well-corseted stomach. 'And I have a something blue to every room. For the Evil Eyes. Each plate and lamp has made me a hundred steps to climbing before I find, and I am not pleased for the Evil Eyes to make them smithering. Ah no! There is too many Evil Eyes here.'

Perhaps we should have organised a 'something blue' to protect *our* house. We have not yet progressed far beyond bare white walls and the absolute necessities for living, but things are already beginning to smithering.

It is now apparent that every one of the two hundred and forty panes of glass will have to be re-puttied. The original putty is crumbled to a grey powder, and the panes are held only by a tack or two or by globs of fossilised paint. Every time a shutter bangs there is a pretty tinkling of broken glass. The shutters bang constantly because the catches are broken. So there must also be new catches.

'It is nothing, George … nothing! A few thousand *drachmae* will set everything in order. You will have the finest house on the island — well, the best bargain, anyway.'

But, also, 'The Best Niagara' is leaking already. One has always suspected that plumbing was not a strong point with Greek workmen, but it does seem a little soon to have to start repairs. And obviously something will have to be done about the open drain that meanders from the kitchen sink across the courtyard. It disappears under the back gate and apparently continues under the street outside, but there must be a blockage because for the last week the water has not run away, and mosquitoes are beginning to breed in a stagnant, smelly pool.

Lefteri is called in to investigate.

'Where does the water *go*, Lefteri?'

Lefteri gives that maddening shrug. 'Who knows? Perhaps here, perhaps there. I will go outside and dig up the street a little.'

By four in the afternoon he has dug as far as the well in the square. There is a long, twisting trench flanked by uprooted cobblestones and mountains of soil in which twenty children are playing. All the neighbouring women are bringing their buckets to take the soil away for their trees and flower-pots.

There is no sign of a drain.

Perhaps — one is smitten by the thought — the water just seeps into the well? And if the kitchen water seeps into the well, what about the contents of 'The Best Niagara'? Typhoid! Cholera! Amoebic dysentery! Should one raise an alarm? Warn the women who come to the well? See the mayor?

'Po-po-po-po,' says Lefteri consolingly, 'don't you be worried now. I will just buy a few bags of cement and make you a little drain a few metres away from your house, and then I'll cover it all up nicely and we'll say no more about it. Is it *your* business to know where the drainage goes?'

But it takes him two days to make the little bit of a drain and cement down all the cobbles of the street again, and for this we pay another thousand *drachmae*, and are still left wondering what horrors might not be oozing aimlessly under our very foundations and whether when the plague strikes we will be culpable.

Now one winces if a piece of plaster falls, and speaks in a very tight controlled voice to the children playing in the square outside. Since we have come to live here the square has become the favourite playing area for a mile around. For games of chase our front door is 'home': the fresh paint is already scored and scratched, the whitewash is kicked off in patches, and there are many legends written in chalk and pencil to the height of small stretched arms — the names and arrows and accusations and stickmen which form the incomprehensible *graffiti* of the very young.

It will all need to be done again, with good paint at forty-four *drachmae* the small can.

It is with surprise and dismay that I catch the tone of my own voice admonishing the children a dozen times a day, and recognise in myself the shrewish housewife who keeps the parlour locked and lays a newspaper trail so the floors will not be soiled. Like T. S. Eliot's lady: 'That isn't what I meant at all. That isn't it at all.'

But I see now just how right Henry was on that first day when we all inspected the house together and he sat in the window embrasure and said '... it's best like this.' And, in a way, so it was — the old house, still, dark, secret, odorous, waiting. What pleasure one had had in thinking, here I will make something very beautiful, here will be cleanliness and order and warmth and comfort, here where there is only an old dilapidated house there will be a home, a refuge, and my own light will shine on my own bit of creation.

How far away yet is any such achievement. Already we have paid out thousands of *drachmae* over and above the purchase price of the house, and yet for negative gains. How much easier it used to be to berate a landlord if the roof leaked or the drains proved unfunctional!

'Still,' George said one morning at breakfast, 'it is rather wonderful, after all, to see the fruit ripening on your own trees, and to know that your children after you will see them in the same season. Security, permanence ...' And even as he spoke there was an ear-splitting crack from the garden where a collection of gigantic alley tomcats had cornered a slit-eared female on a branch of our lemon tree. George's howl of fury rose about the howls of the cats scampering over the garden wall. The lemon tree was split quite in halves!

'Perhaps we can splint it,' I said dismally, surveying the sad wreckage of leaves and twigs and little green lemons, small as almonds, and the gaping wound in the trunk of the tree. 'If we rope it up and putty it, and put a big prop under this fallen branch, maybe it might heal ...'

But George had begun to howl again, crowned with lemon leaves and shaking branches in both hands like a demented Druid invoking wrathful, punitive powers.

'Jesus God! Look at the plum tree!' he screamed. 'Look at the bloody plum tree! It's *stripped*!'

And so, alas, it was. Of the heavy crop of fruit which we had watched ripening with pride and satisfaction (preserves, I had thought, plum pies, jars of jam, baskets to be carried to Lola and Zoë and Kyria Heleni and Little Cuckoo) there was one single yellow fruit left hanging on the topmost bough. And though George raged and stamped and swore he would send for the police, would beat every child in the neighbourhood about the ears, would drown his own, would murder all bloody cats — there was nothing we could do. The house had been empty for many, many years, and the fruit crop had been the prize for whoever could clamber over the wall. The fact that now the house is occupied is not enough to make the local children tamely relinquish their rights; the plums will taste all the sweeter for the additional spice of peril. (How one's heart had beat wildly in the dark, how high the wall had seemed and one's knickers tearing as one had scrambled on to the first bough, and then the whispers and bursts of stifled laughter, the snatchings and tuggings at the half-seen, half-felt fruit, the stuffings into a hastily gathered pinafore, and then the sharing, breathless with terror and wild running, and how sweet the juice running down one's mouth in the dark and ambrosial the stolen squelchy flesh that they always told you had worms in it, and you couldn't see and were sick in the paddock thinking of the worms slithering down into your belly and suddenly feeling them in your mouth ... 'That's all very well,' replies my new peevish property-owner's voice, 'but this is *different*.')

Then there is the fact that Dionyssos has not called for the garbage for two weeks. ('Oh, *he's* just great! Just natural. So drunk and so happy. You wouldn't want him to *work*, would you? Come on now, you couldn't really want to destroy a truly joyous soul ... a real natural?' Thus Sykes Horowitz.) To hell with Sykes Horowitz. The garbage cans are beginning to stink. The garden is overrun by a plague of black beetles. The dog has dug up the nasturtium patch again. ('I'll murder that bloody dog! I'll *murder* him!' Thus George.) And Martin's mattress is found to have bed bugs in it.

Kyria Heleni, summoned in to identify the little musky black creature squashed bloodily on the sheet, says there's no doubt. It's a bug all right.

'Funny,' she adds hurriedly, 'I've never had a single one in *my* house, ever. Come to think of it, I don't think I've ever seen a bug before.'

'Well, burn the mattress anyway,' says George. 'Let's be on the safe side.'

'Mother of God!' Kyria Heleni throws up her hands in consternation. 'You don't have to do that! A little *schoni* sprinkled on ... just wait a bit, I think I just might have a packet in the house ...'

For a woman of the laity so far as bed bugs are concerned, she is certainly incredibly expert at de-bugging a mattress. My own feeling is that the mattress ought to be burnt, but then there is the restraining thought that a new one will cost another three hundred *drachmae*. Now we are all creepy and twitchy and filled with horror.

The baby's basket is found to have bugs too.

'That isn't what I meant at all. That isn't it at all!'

From a real adversary courage flows into you. But there is no lifting of the heart when all you are asked to fight are bed bugs and garbage cans and stinking drains. Even to keep even a semblance of order in such a big house is an all-day job. Upstairs and downstairs, to sweep, to pick up children's litter, to tidy, to ferret out dust ... marketing, making meals, cleaning up after them ... the baby needs attention, the pot is boiling over, the kerosene stove has blown up in your face again, Shane can't find her clean socks, your hands are covered with charcoal and no water in the tap — and that damned old woman is lumbering into the kitchen again, tapping with her staff!

'Health and joy, my child! Where is Sophia?'

What creativeness in this? Here is no progression, no building towards some ideal summit, but only a perpetuation of the present. The clean becomes soiled, one makes the soiled clean, the clean becomes soiled again. One is as weary as a gladiator after combat, and yet tomorrow will bring no rest. All is to be done again, and yet again. And was it for this, I think, examining my grimed hands ruefully, that I renounced so gladly the material comforts of civilisation? The gadgets? The labour-saving devices? The advantages of technological progress? The hot-water supply? The telephoned shopping list? The Mister Stork Nappy-Wash? The escape hatches of pretty clothes, lotions, French perfumes, theatres, concerts, cocktails, idle window shopping?

A housewife is a housewife wherever she is — in the biggest city of the world or on a small Greek island. There is no escape. She must move always to the dreary recurring decimal of her rites.

George too has problems, but of a different sort. In actual fear of poverty for the first time in his adult life he is doomed to write not what he *wants* to write but what he knows will sell. For him, creative freedom is still a will-o'-the-wisp. He is bound to provide for the wants of a whole family. His life is bound to theirs, to four separate individuals all with abundant life of their own, but for whom his life is a necessity: his very thoughts must be conditioned by their needs. Battling through mornings made mad with infestations of curious neighbours, the exasperating continuing visits of old Mrs Silk looking for the shade of Sophia, the problems of choked drains and splitting lemon trees, anxiously watching the post, examining the bankbook, he must often think ... Was it for this that I so gladly renounced the pleasures of material success? The assurance of the monthly cheque? The visible achievements? The automobile, the well-dressed wife, the comfortable apartment at a 'good' address, the tidy, well-mannered children going to tidy, well-mannered schools?

Yes, but how grey it all was, and how the days stretched out ahead like a flat leaden plain, each so like the other, sterile, meaningless, and how one was filled with a nameless dread hurrying faster and ever faster on through the grey safe days, on with the unquestioning herd. For what would happen if one was left behind?

Ask nothing of it and the soul retires, the flame of life flickers, burns lower, expires for want of air. Here, in the midst of all our difficulties, life burns high. Though it seems sometimes that we make no progress towards the ideal, yet the ideal *exists*, and our energies are directed towards it. The very presence of these three eager living little creatures reminds us that we are committed to life: this house — so bare yet — is an affirmative statement. Living simply, living in the sun, we are at least in touch again with reality; we have bridged that chasm that separates modern life from life's beginnings and come back to the magic and wonder of such sensible mysteries as fire, water, earth, and air. And, more than this, we have no masters but ourselves.

Our position among the other expatriate protestants who are also seeking to take their lives back into their own hands is a curious one. In a particular way, we are unique. By them we are regarded as being successful. We own a house, support a family, and have books actually published. But also, to them, we embody that very dull normality from which they are all fleeing. We are respectable revolutionaries, often heavy with responsibilities, harassed by children, and apparently less concerned with the state of our psyches than with the state of our drains.

Feodor is contemptuous, but covertly, for he needs often to borrow money. Obviously he has a deeply held conviction that those who are so insensitive as to bend their labours towards the end of bread-and-butter owe a share of it to those who live for Art alone.

Unheralded by so much as a knock, he shambles straight up the stairs to the studio, leaving a trail of spit and clay on the fresh white paint. It is difficult to believe that he is not yet thirty. His skin has a soggy texture, his beard is thin and straggling and already flecked with grey, his nostrils are pinched, his little, bleary, goaty eyes sunk deep in their sockets. His body gives off an odour that is part rank goatiness and part decaying vegetable matter. He looks sick. A sick goat. An imbecile goat.

'Tzorj! My friend Tzorj!'

'Well,' says my friend Tzorj with a certain grimness, 'if it isn't Dorian Grey!'

'Excuse me, eh? I make some things for the children, no.' And he holds up two pottery mugs, phallic in design and very clumsily executed. 'I am a genius, no?'

'No,' says my friend Tzorj.

Feodor gives an incredulous honk of laughter. 'You do not *like*?'

'No,' says my friend Tzorj. 'And if my children even touched them I'd scrub them with carbolic.'

Then Feodor begins to sniffle a bit, for it is the lot of genius to be misunderstood and unloved. And he is an aristocrat, of grande delicatesse, who has given his soul to Art! He pulls his pocket inside out, and peers at it in disbelief. 'Lola and Sean do not love me either,' he says sulkily, with a whine creeping into his voice. 'I behave with grande delicatesse, I degrade myself in politesse. I smoke their cigarette butts. *I!* I could turn them out

111

of my house. I could charge them rent. But no! I am above such bourgeois conceptions. I have the *noblesse oblige*. And for this I am insulted. They lock up the wine and hide the housekeeping purse!'

Visits from Feodor generally cost from ten to fifty *drachmae*, according to the duration of the visit, and the quality, size, and obscenity of the cracked clay offering. George, I think, is working on the theory that since Feodor will never be able to repay the money he will gradually begin to avoid us. George has these moments of innocence. He cannot see that Feodor is working on the theory that it is really George who owes *him* money. For I have observed Feodor, after he has concluded his profusion of thanks for the loan and having expressed suitable sentiments of esteem and admiration for ourselves and our children ... I have seen Feodor shamble down the stairs, spit deliberately on the doorstep, break wind loudly, and with a gesture embracing the house by the well, all its occupants and their several aspirations, mutter in a tone of unutterable scorn, '*Banality!*'

Sykes Horowitz, on the other hand, comes to visit with his best foot self-consciously forward and his best manners brushed up for the occasion. He is at once diffident, respectful, and exhibitionist. We are definitely 'in the family', but rather in the category of respectable maiden aunts of means but little worldly knowledge, who have yet to learn the facts of life.

'Gee, it sure is great to be in a home again,' he says with a sigh. At the same time he manages to convey his impression that we lead dull, sheltered, unadventurous lives, and that if he liked he could really raise our hair. He hints at depravities, at experiences undreamed of in our normal existence. His eyes wander restlessly, he smokes with quick, nervous inhalations, and his quiet, jerky voice goes on and on in little spurts and rushes about traumas and psychosomatic disorders and meeting Rilke's wife and dancing naked in a bar in Munich and meeting a man in Stockholm who wanted him to replace a suicide. It is all very difficult to follow, since he never begins or ends a sentence or ever quite formulates an idea, and his language is a confusing mixture of deliberately old-fashioned American slang, psychiatric jargon, jazz terms, and French quotations. Yet one is aware of a real intensity behind what he is saying. He is trying desperately to make you understand something. Constantly he seems to be jerking back from the brink of a confession, a confession the ghastliness of which appals him ... so that his conversation is punctuated with these abrupt pauses which he fills in with a mock-confused, 'Gee, but I couldn't tell *you* about *that!*'

Yet behind his surface need to be admired for admiring Rilke and Kierkegaard, to be an object of titillated wonder for the depth of his experience, and of sympathy for the extent and variety of his traumas, abnormalities, and psychosomatic disorders, one registers very clearly the man's painful, aching need to be liked just for himself, to be accepted as a whole human being, to find someone, anyone, to believe what he wants so desperately to believe himself — that he is sincere, purposeful, and dedicated, and that he is actually going to start to paint tomorrow.

'Funny, I just can't pin down the mood in this place. I drink and drink. Do you think I ought to go up to Athens for a bit and have a real orgy? Maybe I could work then. I don't know. Money, too — that's a problem. God, this island certainly is *dead*. Europe is rotten though, isn't it? George, how the hell do you manage to work every day?'

George grins: 'Three children to support.'

'Sure, sure! It's tough being tied like that. My God, my parents are awful. They don't think much of me. A hundred dollars a month, that's what they send me. A hundred lousy bucks, and then I have a patron who sends me a cheque now and then. You couldn't lend me fifty drachs I suppose until my allowance comes? I still haven't bought any paints and I'm just wild to get *started*. Owed all the last allowance around the town for food and drink. God, how I envy you people who are *integrated*!'

And one notices, with a little pang of sorrow, that his close-cropped black hair is speckled all over with grey, and there is white in the stubble of unshaven beard on his jowls, and under it his chin sags perceptibly. Ten years and more have passed since he first brought his gifts to lay worshipfully at the culture-cradle of the Left Bank, and for all those years he has been credulously swallowing a religion of despair created by and for an older, wearier, stronger-stomached race than his. And where is he to look for hope now? The habit of despair is strong, and even if he should actually begin to paint tomorrow he must surely be aware that all his drives are imitative now and his labours doomed to barrenness, and that for him it is too late to begin again. The gifts have tarnished long ago.

How much more gracefully and easily does Jacques interpret precisely the same religion to suit his needs. It permits him to live as he pleases, and he asks nothing more of it. And to live as he pleases is to live as most young men would please, to be irresponsible, completely untroubled by guilt or conscience, to behave just as it suits one at the particular moment, to have unlimited licence to be rude to one's elders and betters, to cock a defiant snook at convention, morality, dullness, law and order, progress, rectitude, and occasionally to wear a mood of *angst* like an interesting accessory that will point up the radiance, the boundless confidence, the wonderful abundant *livingness* of youth and beauty. One wonders if it will suit him so well when *his* jaw begins to sag and there is a bald spot in that thick gold hair.

"Ullo,' he says, sidling in through the kitchen door and squatting down on the stone floor, a sprig of jasmine tucked behind his ear. 'Do you think you might lend me fifty *drachmae*? I gave all the money I'ad to Feodor, and now I don't have any to take Toto to the Poison Pit for dinner.'

There is a new furrow of thought creasing George's forehead these days.

'It isn't that I'm mean, or even that I mind being thought respectable, but I'm just beginning to wonder if I'm expected to bloody well subsidise them *all*!'

3

We had just rounded the cliff path above the cave when we met Sean and Lola, both sweating profusely and hung all about with bundles and cases and baskets. Behind them Andonis was leading two mules, also laden with baggage.

'Did you see Socrates in the *agora*? We have to find another house!'

'But what on earth has happened?'

Sean eased down his bundles and lowered himself carefully on to a flat rock. 'Feodor,' he said, 'has *broken out*.'

There had been an atmosphere of strain developing for some time, Sean explained. Not only were Feodor's personal habits hard to bear, but he never cleaned up his own messes. He and Sykes had been out dynamiting fish at night with some of the local fishermen, and then getting drunk in obscure taverns and grocery shops, and finally Feodor had, with great *noblesse oblige*, taken to asking all the fishermen home and giving parties with Lola's wine and provisions. The bouts of remorse which always followed were even harder to bear. Then he had found an old army medical kit filled with stale miracle drugs, and had started pumping the credulous neighbours full of penicillin and streptomycin.

'But he hasn't started operating yet?' I asked, recalling the case of blunt surgical instruments with which he had arrived on the island.

'Oh yes, he has,' said Sean. 'But only on tomcats. The *dirrrrty* bastard!'

The final blow had been the arrival of the woodman that morning, imperatively demanding of Lola that she pay for the two loads of wood delivered to their house for the pottery oven.

'So,' said Lola, 'we packed our things and left.'

'What is Feodor doing now?'

'Committing suicide,' said Sean. 'I hope.'

Two days later, as we brushed past the young fig tree and turned down the path, we came upon Lola straddling a rock and shouting wild abuse in English down to the water below.

'Goths!' she screamed. 'Vandals! Bloody barbarians! Just look down there. *Look!* Just look down there and see what they're doing!'

There was a small grey naval craft moored by the long rock, and two groups of sailors, one on the shore and one in a dinghy, were hauling into position a huge iron net that stretched from the end of the long rock back to the furthermost tip of the bottom sunbathing platform. A small triangle of water was thus enclosed immediately in front of the cave. All along the top of the net were affixed great empty black drums, sinister-looking things like floating mines, that clanged together with a grim, hollow, melancholy sound.

'But what is it for?'

'Sharks,' a sailor said simply, and snapped his teeth together.

4

And after all we go on swimming at the cave. Even with the hideous net it is still the most beautiful place, and for us, who never have more than an hour or so free, it is the only place we can reach conveniently and still have time to swim.

Besides, that word *shark* has been let loose, and it drifts about now and drops suddenly into thought and conversation. A shadow or a patch of weed waving on the sea floor is now imbued with menace; one breaks surface and speeds for the shore. It seems a little silly that the children are now confined within the net when a week ago they were swimming a hundred metres out, but somehow I dare not give them permission to swim outside. For it is true that the fishermen have netted two sharks recently in the channel where the *Sirina* runs down the coast, and they have pointed out that the cave is only a couple of hundred metres away from the slaughterhouse, where twice a week the guts and entrails and blood of slaughtered beasts are thrown into the sea.

Worse almost than the threat of sharks though is the tangible nuisance of a group of about a dozen young men, labourers around the port, who congregate at the cave whenever any foreigners are swimming there. They all have EOKA stencilled or embroidered across the fronts of their bathing pants and behave with undisguised lewdness. Apart from that, they delight in jumping from the cave lip, all together, whenever someone is swimming underneath, with their hands clasped about their knees as they hit the water to make the impact as violent as possible. It is not specially dangerous, unless one of them actually jumps right on an unsuspecting swimmer, but it is stupid and annoying.

One of the saddest by-products of this Cyprus business, as far as I can see, is that it has given moral licence to small boys and loutish adolescents to indulge their instincts for exhibitionism, persecution, and torment. Normally they would only tear newborn kittens limb from limb or torture stray dogs.

We are still free from persecution — in fact, the kindness of the islanders to us is still overwhelming — but all the other foreign residents, whatever their nationalities, are tormented in some degree, mostly by small boys who throw stones and shout catchcries they don't understand.

Ironically, the worst sufferers are Hippolyte and Jacques who, both being French, have nothing whatever to do with the Cyprus issue. Hippolyte, who is normally very fond of small boys, is now seen almost every day heading towards the police station in a nervous frenzy, dragging some howling, shaven boy behind him, firmly held by the ear. This, of course, only results in more stones, and really vindictive persecution. Hippolyte swears he will leave the island. We suggest that perhaps if he left off his pink shell necklace and his Riviera shirt … or just tried to ignore the children … or even emulated Jacques, who cuffs with a rather startling savagery whenever he can lay his hands on one. Cassandra says her Aunt Theodore reports that Jacques now has a skull and crossbones painted on his door and underneath it, neatly lettered in Greek, 'I eat children.' Cassandra is deeply horrified.

Arriving tourists tell of all sorts of persecutions in Athens: I suspect willing drama into incidents that were probably no more than rudeness. On the island here the café proprietors and restaurant owners are deeply concerned because the tourists are yet so few, and then mostly French and German, who, at the best of times, are niggardly spenders. Old Stamatis, stringing his lead sinkers at the back of the shop, snorts at the wax dummy, 'That girl of mine will ruin us with her nonsense!'

Still, weekends are gay with parties of Athenians, and there is a fair smattering of artists up at the school — French, Swedish, and German ... no English this year, nor Americans.

Maiden ladies in cotton dresses and coolie hats have their easels set up along the waterfront or at various vantage points on the clifftops. The German girls are more industrious than ever, particularly the youngest one, but although her head is bowed over her sketchblock and her pencil indefatigably records houses, boats, café tables, donkeys, peasant women, and old fishermen at the rate of dozens a day, one senses that her heart is not in them at all. Her eyes are often red with weeping and her two companions look smug. Jacques is gathering limpets these days in some private cove far along the cliffs, and gathering limpets with him is a big, husky-voiced Athenian girl. Cassandra's Aunt Theodora reports 'Par Epano' twanging out until four in the morning. The woman who lives in the lower half of the house has complained that the creaking of the floorboards wakes up her baby.

Pepsin, Strepsin, and Amylopsin are to return to Sweden.

'We have stayed long already away.'

'We have enjoyed it most well.'

'But we have no more money.'

'I'm going away too,' says Hippolyte. 'I cannot stand these louts gibbering and shrieking at me any more. I am frightened. But really I am terrified. Heaven knows *what* they would do to me if they caught me alone.' And in actuality he is really frightened: it would be comic if it were not so genuine. He is really afraid that if he is found alone he will be subjected to physical violence. Twice he has come at night to sleep on our divan because he dared not go home alone late at night, and at the cave he has been practising ju-jitsu.

But Jacques, sniffing delicately at his spray of jasmine, takes his feet off the table and scratches his bare heel thoughtfully. With complete and terrifying sincerity he snarls briefly, 'Why don't you bash their bloody 'eads in?'

5

Yet living has become infinitely more pleasant and less complicated now in summer.

Imperceptibly one relaxes more and more, and there are queer moments when time telescopes and in some scrap or fragment of ordinary domestic usage — a salt-stiff bathing suit strung on a line, a straw hat hanging on a nail, sweet red cherries heaped in a wooden bowl, a clock ticking, a kicked-off sandal, salad vegetables crisping in an enamel pail, a sprig of mint crushed between the fingers — one enters again, with an aching sense of wonder, the bright, lost world of one's own childhood.

Outside in the garden the sun strikes sharp as a sword; it is only early in the morning that I can put the baby out under the splinted and bandaged lemon tree, where he lies browning in his basket like a joint in the oven. The plums are lost to us, but the vines are hung with tight little bunches of grapes like tiny clusters of green beads, and I can cut basketsful of tender leaves to make *dolmadhes*. The mint and parsley are standing high and strong, the geraniums have burst into lolly-pink bouquets, very stiff and Victorian among the round green leaves, and the succulents that I planted before we moved house are beginning to creep over the wall.

Inside the kitchen it is dark and cool; one is glad of thick stone walls, smooth stone floors that are glassy and cold to the touch of bare feet, the damp, ribbed water jars where the ferns are beginning to twine.

While I work I can hear the dull thudding of George's typewriter up in the studio — that familiar intermittent chatter that has been the background to all my married life, and the children chanting their alpha-beta. Sing-song and hypnotic it comes from the Down School and breaks finally into a charming and innocent-sounding rendering of the newest revolutionary Cyprus song.

The whole domestic mechanism seems to run more easily in these long blue days. Marketing is a joy, meals easy to prepare, clothes no problem, the children are happy and absorbed in their own rich, fantastic world of growing and learning and playing and living, the baby has settled into a model routine in spite of the neighbours, and there is always time for swimming in the afternoon — the daily never-failing magic of the gulf and the islets; and the clear green sea.

Then in the evening how pleasant it is to stroll down to the waterfront through narrow lanes where the scent of summer flowers hangs so sweet and heavy as to be almost visible: the sweet, white, heavy summer flowers, jasmine and gardenias and fooli and thick white stocks that breathe their sweetness into the night from courtyards hidden behind high white garden walls. Even the tables on the waterfront have jam jars filled with stock and gardenias, and the scent of the flowers breathes and blends with the smell of hot rocks and salt and herbs and fish frying in olive oil.

The café tables are all ranked along the waterfront by the sea, blocks of white plastic tablecloths or checked gingham ones, arranged in rows under loops of naked electric light bulbs. The restaurants are gay in new paint, bright and open. From Johnny Lulu's comes the scritch and wail of a *bouzouki* record and in a cleared space between the tables some young men in blue jerseys are dancing the slow, controlled, balancing dance of the island, with their knees pressed tightly inwards and their trouser legs twitched together delicately with two fingers. Slow, slavish, monotonous the dance; the absorbed faces of the young men never look up; their protruding bottoms jerk spasmodically like nautch girls' to the spasmodic snapping of their outstretched fingers. Bottom, crutch, feet, moving to a slow, secret, private rhythm ...

Between the open restaurants and the tables by the sea the evening promenade passes and repasses, formally respectable.

Here on the waterfront there is always company. It is easy to join a group around a plastic tablecloth and a flask of wine, and to sit for hours, gossiping, watching the evening promenade go by, conscious that one's skin is still salty and one's hair still damp from swimming, that one's limbs are relaxed, that one is not really attentive at all. Chitter, chatter, chitter, the conversation spurts and falls and chitters on again, idle, derisive, malicious — summer talk. Feodor is to be run off the island ... Hippolyte has found an adelphic friend and my God you should see the little monster ... do you know what Mitzo sells in those cigarette tins he keeps on the top shelf? Did you hear that the handyman of a certain wealthy lady was seen climbing the stairs to Jacques' house with a basket of fresh eggs? Sykes has a complaint that he says is psychosomatic — but if you ask *me* ... Toby Nicholls has gone and bought a bloody great loom for that poor girl Katharine, and now she has to learn weaving ...

Chitter, chitter, chitter ... and outside the brilliant circle of the electric globe, the dark water laps and laps with the soft swish of silk and the night presses down around the town, warm and close like a cloak, soft as velvet, heavy with salt and the scent of white flowers.

July

I

Our royalty statements have come in and we must accept the fact that we are caught. Far from taking a holiday in Venice, even a trip to Athens is out of the question. The garden terraces we had planned will have to wait, the new trellises for the vines, the built-in cupboards, the bookshelves for the studio. As for the boat, that raft of dreams that has expanded curiously through months of talk and wishing, from a summer dinghy to a converted sponge caique in which we were to sail right up into the Black Sea following the route of Jason's *Argo*, it has drifted back, 'a swan asleep', into the rosy anchorage of Cloud Cuckoo Land, together with Flecker's Old Ships, Cleopatra's Barge, and the Quinquereme of Nineveh.

Now, what a curious effect this chill blast has had upon us.

On the surface of it, the situation is unchanged. We are poor, but then we have been poor for the last two years — poorer, indeed, than we are now, with a house of our own, and enough money to live for another six months or so even if we should earn nothing more. Those two years of poverty have been the most eventful, the most enjoyable, the most exciting of our lives; we have felt richly defiant and adventurous eating lentils and wearing darned sweaters and thumbing our noses at the jeremiahs who had said we couldn't do it. So why should one now have a hard knot in one's heart — not so much of fear, but of outrage, of the wildest indignation? What is this protesting cry of anger and disbelief that wells up in one's throat? Why, it is very simple. It is only that one has come face to face with the plain bleak realisation that perhaps *we are to go on being poor*!

We can maintain the situation, hold the fort, provide a home and food, but what effort even so much has cost already and will cost yet — only to maintain — and perhaps ... the dismaying thought has to be faced ... perhaps there is to be *nothing more*! Dear God, what a world of difference there is, after all, in living simply because you choose to do so and living simply because you must!

Caught. Marooned. Incredulously we try to accept the fact that we really *are* marooned, castaways on a little rock. True, the rock is very pretty, the company is gay and amusing, the life healthy. Nobody could cavil at the abundance, the variety, the cheapness of the summer foods piled and heaped and spilling from every stall along the cobbled waterfront. Such melons and peaches and apricots, such peppers and little green squashes and purple aubergines and tomatoes the size of your two fists. Why, one can live on next to nothing, and live well too. Then what imp of perversity is it that makes me long for asparagus, for mushrooms, for tender-loin steaks, and château-bottled claret?

Did I say I was glad to be committed? What ignorant chittering. Sometimes, looking out at noon at the brazen, clanging mountains, I am secretly appalled. It is a terrible landscape. Mummified by heat, all the juices dried out of it, naked, hairless country. Weakly, I long for the soft deception of trees and grass, cool rivers, for the asphalt crust of city streets, for cinemas, taxi-cabs, neon lights, meaningless clamour, or even just a box of good expensive make-up. At least let me cover my naked face with an illusion!

For how very different even our actual physical selves appear to be now. It is an aspect which one had not given much thought to — we looked shabby perhaps, but very fit and suntanned. Well, we *are* suntanned, but how scraggily thin we are, how nervous, and what an astonishing number of new lines there are, tension lines, worry lines, that are scored deeply and for all time.

Our clothes, beaten for two years now on stones or rubbed to a pulp in flat tin tubs, have faded to anonymous colours, sun colours, pebble colours … and not a garment among us but has a variegated pattern of dams and patches or is held together by pins or bits of string. I am not complaining of this. One develops a curious snobbery about old clothes, and Cassandra does launder them as beautifully as if they were fresh from the boxes and tissue paper of Bond Street. But I had not realised how truly awful they are, nor how truly awful we must all look — George with his long, deeply scored face crowned by a semi-crewcut that has been done with the kitchen shears and looks it, me with my tattered shirts, ancient skirts, sandals that are reduced to one knotted strip of leather holding on a frayed sole, and my hair grown long, lank, and stiff with salt. The horrible conclusion dawns that we look just as 'eccentric', just as tritely 'bohemian', as goaty Feodor, or Jacques with his affected apache clothes and his gold earring.

And where has our patience gone, our good humour? We are nervous, inclined to irritability, to sudden explosions of violence; we are captious, querulous, and tired. Other people's problems no longer arouse the least sympathy, nor even interest. When Sykes looks up with his miserable lost-dog eyes from the spit-and-crayon abstract he is making publicly outside a coffee house and begins, with self-conscious diffidence, to quote Gertrude Stein on 'the lost generation', one feels only a bitchy resentment. Damn it all, one thinks angrily, all that was thirty years ago! This is a grown man with a private income, talent, and no responsibilities. What the hell is *he* crabbing about? Let him work out his own salvation, or drink himself to death, whichever is the quicker. Even the sight of Feodor is unbearable. There's a bit of honest-to-God degradation, disintegration — choose whichever word you want — if you like! He even smells of corruption. Well, let him rot. He'll rot just as fast without subsidies from us. And Jacques. Jacques too. How offensive, how artificial and silly his provocative, shuffling walk, his skin-tight pants, his jasmine flower, and that damned earring. How intentional it all is — the slow eyelids, the enigmatic smile, the shirt arranged to display the better the golden mat of hair on breast and belly, the irresistible glance that flicks on and off like a traffic light, the interesting touch of *angst*. Not Dionysos after all, the fleet, the free, the beautiful, the ever-young — but only a little curly dog in season, whose imperative it is to sniff after any and every lady dog.

Are these our spiritual brothers? For they, too, have protested, made a definite stand, refused to submit, declared for individuality, and retired from the rat race. We all talk the same language, have more or less the same culture pattern, the same frame of reference. We laugh at the same jokes, understand the same implications in events, and are equally perturbed at the trend of modern civilisation. We are here, all together, on the same small island, living more or less the same way, and looking — alas! — most definitely A Foreign Group, variations on a theme of escapism.

Yet I refuse to acknowledge them my spiritual brothers. For they have declared not only against the rat race of modern life, but against life itself. The human race, they say, is an irremediable disaster, the heavens and earth a conjoined imbecility, life itself nothing but a torture chamber of senseless affliction. And saying this they absolve themselves from all responsibility, all control, all moral laws, all sense of duty. Humility is lacking in them. They know no direction. They have lost all sense of wonder.

So between us there lies a subtle antagonism, always present, always gnawing in the way of a sore tooth that one must prod with one's tongue, curiously attractive and not to be let alone. Not that one *could* let it alone even if one would. For there is only one waterfront, one little hoop of cobbles, and at night there is nowhere else to go. It has come to be an arena, or a stage, so theatrically picturesque it is, so intentionally lit with loops of light, and the ranks of tables waiting ...

Inevitably we all meet again, and yet again. We are endlessly meeting ... the same people over and over again, endlessly meeting. Sean and Lola, George and I, Hippolyte, Sykes, Jacques, Feodor, odd additions and subtractions according to the tourist traffic and the state of Jacques' amours. Within the group there is fluctuation, but the plastic tablecloth is eternal, the cold stuffed tomatoes or the cold fish congealing on the plate, the scarred, evil, scrofulous cats scavenging around one's feet, the carafe of pale yellow wine replenished again and again, the eternal conversation. Always the same conversation, yesterday, today, tomorrow, the same smart verbal catch-ball with obscure poets and philosophers, the same Freudian terms, the same 'frank' piggery, the same little shafts of malice and spite, the same derisive laughter.

Warm, mad, and wonderful the nights, wearing the soft bloom of purple grapes. The water lapping dark, and a huge mad moon extinguishing behind the sharp mountain edges like every dream one ever had. What are we doing here under the mad moon watching the promenade pass and repass — the linked girls, the complacent citizens, the gay tourists, the self-conscious artists, the few groups of aristocrats come down from their lofty places to mingle with the village people? They all have their places. They belong. Why did we have to protest, burn our bridges, isolate ourselves, strip off our protective colouring as if it had been a decontamination suit? Why? Just to sit eternally and eternally around the plastic tablecloth playing verbal pitch and toss, baiting, being baited, being bored, drinking too much wine, becoming too angry or too tired to stop.

'Let's go on! Let's go somewhere else!' someone cries gaily. 'There's music tonight in Yanni's *taverna*. Let's go and drink some more and dance.'

But we must get up so early in the morning, we demur. There is the baby. We've got a lot of work on hand at the moment.

'Oh, come *on*!' They are already moving. 'Let down your hair for once!' Their smiles are curiously and infinitely pitying, the irresponsible, the uncommitted, who can sleep until noon and then take a swim to clear their fumed heads. They shrug and go off laughing into the night, looking for music, for dancing, for wine and still more wine, while we — proved yet again to be priggish, dull, respectable spoilsports — go home a little drunker than we ought to be, feeling vaguely worsted, jangling with some unspecified resentment, indefinably *tainted*.

Better perhaps to emulate Toby and Katharine Nichols, to live 'Greekly', almost to repudiate one's own language, one's own culture, to deny the existence of one's own kind and try to make reality out of slavish imitation. But then how faintly ludicrous is Toby's Greek moustache, and Katharine's headscarf. How nonsensical the play acting of the wooden loom, the nightly ceremony of lighting the lamp before the *ikons*. And I have a notion that even fanatical determination *and* a private income will not bring off the complete conversion. Katharine has gone back to the gymnasium tutor for her lessons. She seems to have some queer block as far as the Greek language is concerned, Toby reports worriedly: every lesson ends in tears. Love for a country is not enough. Lord Byron, they say, detested the Greeks.

Well, thank God we *are* marooned, that there is no question of going back. If there was a chance of escape I suspect that George might take it. He was never made to fight a holding action. Out and attack for George, and lavish the spoils. It's hard for him to be caught like this. I watch him sometimes hating the mountains. He looks baffled, uneasy, and afraid.

2

And now, when it is siesta time for any purposeful activity, summertime, playtime, easy-living time, lotus-eating time, we must be very purposeful indeed.

The island is wearing its holiday face. The gulf is like milk. There are little motorboats ferrying tourists down the coast to further coves and beaches, there are fishing caiques sliding through their own reflections, market boats skittering across to the mainland to the rumba rhythm of their exhausts, and all the little *várkas* that rested in lanes and sheds for the winter are sprinkled down through the islets like coloured scraps of confetti, or walnut shells painted crimson and cinnamon and lime and yellow and pink; in each an old man standing, rocking dreamily at the oars, and a boy bent over a glass-bottomed tin looking for octopi.

On Saturdays the *Sirina* lists with the weight of weekending Athenians, family parties in funny hats and Gay Young Things carrying spearguns and underwater equipment. The School is packed with artists. Maria is doing a brisk trade in souvenirs. Socrates has abandoned carpentry altogether. He trots up and down the quay in a frenzy of business, losing keys and forgetting appointments and promising impossibilities. Creon has changed into a white suit and white buckskin shoes and sits outside Soteris' coffee house, brusque, businesslike, ready to offer his services as an adviser and interpreter to any foreigner who looks respectable and appears to be in difficulties.

Every weekend our cave is aswarm with girls in bikinis and sleek young men with elaborate underwater equipment. Jacques poses golden on a rock, with his eyelids half-lowered and a jasmine flower in his mouth, deliberating over his next choice of a limpeting companion. A fishing caique slides by with Sykes and Feodor clinging to the rigging, both very drunk. Lola has quite surrendered to the prevailing summer inertia, to days that are filled quite effortlessly with swimming and sleeping and eating, to nights that are occupied with gossip, wine, and the midnight search for obscure taverns where there might be music and dancing. Even Sean has relaxed perceptibly, and now works only in the mornings — 'ah, it's too hot to be purposeful ...' One tries to quell the resentful thought that rises unbidden ... it's all very well for you with a private income and no responsibilities ...

It *is* too hot. From noon until four o'clock all life withdraws and the town shimmers in hot, white silence. We work through siesta because we must, stripped to shorts and streaming rivulets of sweat. The children have finished school until September and live some life of their own: they run more wild than I like but I haven't the time for supervision. I have a theory which I dare not examine too closely, that if I neglect everything just a little I will manage to get most things almost done. The answer to the problem is to ask Cassandra to come every day to look after the house and baby, but we can't really afford full-time help.

'Three hundred a year and a room of one's own,' George quotes Virginia Woolf's writing prerequisite gloomily as he escorts Mrs Silk down the stairs and out the gate. There is a little printed slip pinned above his desk now which reads:

131

' — Virginia Woolf!'

And another on the wall opposite, in tiny whispery letters: 'And Rilke too!' There are also some other favourite injunctions as '*Think!*' and a slogan clipped from a magazine advertisement: 'Make Writing Your *Other* Business!' Today I noticed a new one, biblically inspired. It was obviously scrawled hastily and with passionate feeling:

'A Time to Write and a Time to Puke.'

We never get down to the cave for our swim now until half past five or six o'clock in the evening. And even then it is a rare thing to recapture the old magic. The iron net with its clanging drums on which the EOKA boys sport has made a sort of trap in front of the cave, and the municipal garbage, which is dumped into the sea near the town, drifts down on the current and is captured inside the net. Often one swims, if one can, through decaying melon rinds, rotten tomatoes, cigarette butts, torn paper of all-too-obvious origin, and dubious rubber objects. On slaughtering days the place becomes a horror, for the intestines and offal from the slaughtered goats, sheep, and bulls also drift to the net and for days after hang there rotting in obscene festoons.

'This EOKA-torn, this garbage-haunted sea ...' Sean paraphrases wearily. Across the bland blue water a flotilla of tin cans and vegetable peelings bobs purposefully towards the cave. The EOKA youths don't seem to even notice it, and at weekends I have seen young women in bikinis breaststroking through it disdainfully. But the end for George — 'Christ Almighty! This is the *end*! The last turn of the screw!' was the spectacle of Jacques in his knotted handkerchief, the inevitable jasmine flower in his mouth, floating lazily between a rotted watermelon and a piece of limp white rubber.

This scene has had a profound effect on both George and Sean. It haunts them. They sit together broodingly, making plans to appear on the waterfront with their hair cut *au Jacques*, Sean carrying a small cauliflower head between his teeth, and George wearing a sarong and bangles.

'You too can be cultured ... and *showing* it!' Sean invites George deliriously.

More and more often we swim very early in the morning or very late at night. Before the sun is fairly up, and the world is clean and sparkling (and before Dionyssos has dumped his garbage), we take the children, the baby in his basket, a watermelon, a loaf of fresh bread, and we make breakfast at the cave. At this hour of the day nobody else is ever there. Or at night with Sean and Lola we share crab sandwiches and a flask of red wine, all sprawled companionably in the dark on a sunbathing platform that still holds the day's heat. On the black water the line of iron drums might be the Loch Ness Monster browsing, a tethered kraken that creaks at every movement of its joints and makes moan with a melancholy hollow booming. As we eat our food and drink our wine the talk is intimate again, the half-statements and trailing sentences of people who know they will be understood: one realises that at some time in these passing months we have slipped across the borderline of close acquaintanceship and become friends; one remembers the winter nights in Spiro's window seat, the fine blazing arguments ... there is a nostalgia suddenly for Henry and Ursula. Go on, *fly* then! Bloody well soar, why don't you? There are real things to talk about — the warm comments of *The New Yorker* on Henry's first one-man show in New York, a long article about his work in a London monthly, reproductions of his paintings in a Paris magazine. Will they come back? In the darkness we make conjecture. We hope that Ursula will have her garden, and Henry will have his forge, and that Trojans will clang among the herbaceous borders and the Minotaur roar in the cellar ...

At night the water slides over your body warm and silky, a mysterious element, unresistant, flowing, yet incredibly buoyant. In the dark you slip through it, unquestionably accepting the night's mood of grace and silence, a little drugged with wine, a little spellbound with the night, your body mysterious and pale and silent in the mysterious water, and at your slowly moving feet and hands streaming trails of phosphorescence, like streaming trails of stars. Still streaming stars you climb the dark ladder to the dark rock, shaking showers of stars from your very fingertips, most marvellously and mysteriously renewed and whole again.

3

After rushing down to the pickets with his baggage every day for a week, Hippolyte finally got there in time to catch a boat.

He left tearfully, bound for the Orient, with his pink shell necklace still looped on his bare plucked breast and a portfolio of pretty, pale drawings under his arm. He embraced us all, promised to write, begged us never to forget him.

Rather sadly we mounted the pastel sketch of island houses he had left with us as a farewell gift, and hung it on the end wall of the living room, with Henry's vigorous oil of a market caique and Lola's Chinese-influenced mountains, and a sort of pseudo Klee of the harbour that was a parting gift from an artist we had met last year.

We have all liked Hippolyte and truly wish for him to find happiness and success. But I cannot think that he will discover any solution in the Orient. I can see him with his classic, slightly balding head held determinedly high, and his mouth that should be happy set tightly against a scream of absolute hysteria, rushing eternally along foreign waterfronts and railway stations to catch the one boat or train that will move out so quickly as to leave behind all his misery, his horror, his consuming self-hatred, and the 'here and now' that he finds so unbearable. But 'here' will go with him wherever he goes, and 'now' will change from second to second as fast as he can run, and when he unpacks his baggage at the next foreign port he will only find himself again.

However, lest we forget that his problem exists, the island's foreign transients are now increased by the addition of several other young men who also spend their years in catching boats and trains.

It had never occurred to me before that there must be a whole nomadic tribe of young men which moves across Europe with the changing seasons on a defined trail where the camping places and waterholes are fixed by custom and the big-game areas clearly marked. It is clear, suddenly, that this island is one of the summer camps, a stopover place to rest and exchange stories and information about the year's trail. Something about Sykes Horowitz now becomes much clearer — his odd familiarity with foreign cities and foreign tongues and that gypsyish quality of being at home everywhere and nowhere that used to rather charm me.

For most of these newly arrived young men are also, like Sykes, American — although you would hardly guess it by their accents, which have the careful anonymity of the expatriate with a sedulously acquired stammer added for interest. Their faces have an expatriate anonymity also — interchangeable faces — weary, young-old, vaguely unhealthy under the suntan, and their eyes, like Sykes' eyes, have that same dreadful centre of purposelessness.

They all speak very good French and have a smattering of Italian and Spanish and German and Arabic; they have all met Rilke's wife or Utrillo; they lived next door but one to Wystan Auden on Ischia or Dali on the Costa Brava; at Majorca one summer they had the opportunity to work with Robert Graves; they know Picasso well; they can quote by heart long passages from Gertrude Stein, and Proust and Racine and Kierkegaard and Nietzsche and Baudelaire and Mallarmé; they have read the reviews of the latest books and the latest plays, and talk knowledgeably about action painting, erotic symbols, psychosomatic disorders, the doctrines of nihilism and existentialism, and collage.

They have in common a ready fund of scandalously funny stories involving the great or near-great, and a quick malicious wit that is usually directed against others of their own kind. These particular attributes are so ready and so practised, so smoothly polished, that I suspect they result from long years' experience of having to sing for one's supper. For although all these young men, like Sykes, seem to have some small private income or allowance — they are all, in a way, remittance men —

it is never quite large enough to enable them to live decently but only just enough to make it unnecessary for them to work for a living.

Their years are spent in following a nomadic trail that leads them, as far as I can gather, through Greece to Yugoslavia, to Venice, through Paris to Sweden or down through Madrid to Majorca. Berlin is on the route for some, and for others Beyrout, Tangiers, Casablanca. Various Mediterranean islands are summer camps — Majorca, Ischia, Corsica, Iviza. Capri has been long removed from the list because it is too banal, they say, and also too expensive: there is interested discussion about the possibilities of Elba, of Sardinia, of Pantellaria.

It is quite obvious that this island is gaining in popularity, a summer camp enlivened by shrill cries of greeting and the sharp buzz of malicious stories, a swapping of notes, of names.

Australian swagmen on the road used to have a particular mark that they scratched on the gatepost of any house where they had received food or shelter — a sign to their brethren who came after that a handout might be expected. These intellectual swagmen also mark doors. I know the name of a woman in Venice who can expect to have three unexpected house guests in spring, and a wealthy Stockholm business man catalogued as having a penchant for a certain type of young man ... his personal habits are terribly peculiar, dear, but he *is* always good for a loan ... and there is a nice young couple in Madrid ... bourgeois and apt to be dreary, you know, but if you really get stuck ... and an American lady of certain age and income who has a nice apartment in the Rue du Faubourg St Honore ... if you can *stand* it, I mean. They all appear to be conveniently heterosexual.

Here they usually head first for the School, for they come armed apparently with the necessary papers to prove they are *bona fide* artists, just as they are armed with 'student' concession passes that ensure them reductions on boat and rail fares. Having secured thus a cheap lodging they cast about for someone to provide them with food and drink. There are one or two wealthy elderly women on the island who are wildly superstitious towards artists — the medicine men, the makers of magic symbols — and who can be flattered by the compliments of a good-looking young man. I think Lola's door is also marked. Warmhearted as she is, expansive, garrulous, loving to entertain and be entertained, hungry for news of that Parisian art world where she once studied, she draws the intellectual hoboes like flies to a honeypot. She is disenchanted enough to know that they are singing for their supper, and they know that she knows it. But Lola, aware of the brittleness of it all, is willing to provide the supper for the sake of the song. With her, they are probably at their best, and closest to honesty.

Sykes drops into place now, with Feodor and Jacques, nomads all, although Feodor and Jacques are of the home-grown European variety and have an indefinable air of authenticity that the American young men lack.

In the mornings they sit in front of the coffee houses, writing letters and postcards, or they drift back and forth from the post office, carrying, like Sykes, a volume of poetry, or an old copy of *Perspectives* or *Encounter* or *Partisan Review*. A great deal of their time is occupied with mail — I suppose that in such a way of life it is of paramount importance to keep in touch with information sources and when the mail sacks go up from the *Sirina* there is always a stampede of young, cropped-hair men in blue jeans and bright shirts. Their letters, I have noticed, have sometimes been re-addressed five or six times. They live *poste-restante*.

They haunt me with their young-old, weary, interchangeable faces and their careful accents and their questing, amoral eyes and their scandalously funny stories. We meet them swimming at the cave, sometimes we sit with them on the waterfront at night, or see them drunk in the taverns, dancing a loose parody of the slow, balancing, island dance, gyrating with blind, sick faces on which the good-time grin is stretched and held as though with a strong fixative. It is even difficult to think of any one of them as individual. The boys. The *poste-restante*, interchangeable, culture-addicted, Europe-sick boys, with grey sprinkled through their crewcuts and little pads of drink-fat around their middles, who yearn for the Europe of Gertrude Stein and Scott Fitzgerald and the 'lost generation' of a generation who were losing themselves while they were being born.

They are all more or less of an age with Sykes, the middle thirties and edging over — the war generation who grew up to horror and inherited despair and disillusion. From what they say and don't say around the plastic tablecloth, I gather that they all came to Europe in much the same way as Sykes, carrying their precious little gifts to lay at the shrine. They were to be poets, to be painters, to be writers, come to drink in their culture at the source, the old mystic fountainhead. Perhaps their stomachs weren't strong enough, perhaps their gifts were weighed and found wanting, or perhaps that little private income, the remittance, made it all too easy to put off until tomorrow the actual hard work that might be involved in being the new young prophet.

And now, when they are no longer really young, and Europe is stale old ground, it is too late for them to begin and too late for them to go back. So they go round and round and round, treading the same old beaten track, the clever young men, the witty young men, the careless young men, the oh-so-European young men, the sad young men, who are looking for Gertrude Stein. Do they get frightened, I wonder, as they become staler, and less attractive, and not quite so capable of keeping up with the latest reviews and the latest movements and the screamingly funny stories and the brighter and younger young men? What happens to them when they grow to middle age? When they become old? Is there a special burying ground somewhere, on Ischia or Iviza or Majorca, where their poor peripatetic bones are laid to rest at last? A sort of secret Elephants' Graveyard?

I suggest this to George and he stares at me thoughtfully for a while, but only murmurs in cold distaste, 'The mind *boggles*!'

Thinking of them — and it is impossible not to think of them a good deal — with their tired faces, their fruitless journeyings, their vicarious pleasures, their ersatz culture, their endless self-delusions, one cannot help but contrast them with Henry, who started out on his own nomadic trail at about the same time as they did, with probably an equivalent amount of talent. Henry never had time to learn perfect French nor to acquire a European polish. He was too busy painting, all his energies engaged on the thing he had to say, on his desperation to overcome his own technical shortcomings, on proving his passionate belief that you can fly for the willing of it.

To accomplish anything it is obvious that a talent is not enough. You need a motive, an aim, an incentive, an overwhelming interest be it ambition or fear or curiosity or only the necessity to fill your belly. You need a star to steer by, a cause, a creed, an idea, a passionate attachment. Something must beckon you or nothing is done — something about which you ask no questions.

As if in answer to this thought there is a letter from Henry, scribbled in reply to one of ours that must have conveyed all too clearly our misgivings, our mood of hesitation and incapacity. The message of it comes singing and clear, unequivocal, untinged by doubt. Go on then, *fly*!

4

Athenian friends have come. Gentle Chloe, laden with gifts for the children, and for Lola and me new lipsticks and extravagant flasks of cologne. Wicked old Black John has come too, with his little bird-thin, bird-bright wife Dora, who is descended, they say, from a Byzantine princess, and carries her quick *chic* grey head as if it supported an invisible coronet.

Black John and Dora were preceded by half a caique-load of furniture that was unloaded at the quay and taken by mules to our house. There is a beautiful spidery French desk that belonged to Dora's grandmother, four high-backed carved chairs, a curly buffet with a white marble top, an armchair for George and one of the very rare and lovely old rugs from Arachova.

'Poof!' said Dora. 'We have so much of this old stuff and such a very little apartment. I like to see these things in a big, old house where they belong.'

'Poof!' said Black John. 'It is nothing. You will use these old things until you can buy something better for your own. There, it is very fine. Now we will all have an amusing time together, I think.'

'But,' Dora put in shrewdly, 'I think that you are not so amused now with the island as you used to be. Eh? Why is this? There seems very many funny people here. The time should pass most pleasant.'

Oh, if it were only a matter of being amused, of passing a pleasant summer holiday. For Dora, in spite of post-war poverty, still supports that invisible coronet on her neat grey head and eats only the breast of chicken; she has time to be amused.

It seems there is not to be a bank after all. Hah, says Black John significantly, now I have another bit of business. I have not the interest now to make a bank. Poof! This new affair will be very fine. I will retrieve my finances. You will see. Now, George, if you will just stand at the door of Katsikas' and watch for Dora. Whistle twice if she approaches. I will just go a minute behind the flour sacks and drink a small *mastika*.

But Dora is nowhere on the waterfront, says George. Why not come out and drink your *mastika* in the sunshine? And Black John sighs heavily. The truth is, he says, that he has no pleasure in the stuff if he can drink it openly like everybody else. The pleasure lies in outwitting Dora.

'That John of mine,' sighs Dora with loving sadness. 'He thinks I have no brain in my head. I know what he is doing in the grocery shop. And already he has drunk down all his money and all my money and his father's house and my house and a block of apartment houses and a paper mill. But he looks after me very well in other matters.'

No bank means that we must still go to the next island every time we need to draw money. It is a nuisance and, since one must stay there overnight, costly. This time it is my turn to go, and perhaps because I feel so low I buy a first-class ticket instead of a third-class one. Feeling pleasantly extravagant I climb up the ladder to the *Sirina*'s deck and start up the broad flight of stairs that leads to the sundeck and the luxurious first-class lounge.

I have scarcely set my foot on the stairs before a white-jacketed steward blocks my way.

'First-class up here,' he says curtly. At the same moment I catch a glimpse of myself in the long mirror. Without further protest, without showing him my ticket, I descend to the lower deck and the crates of hens and the old black-shawled women. Had I been the steward I doubt if I would have let me on the boat at all. I feel rather surprised in a detached sort of way, and at the same time quite pleased to have made clear to myself the reason for Chloe's gifts of facecreams and powders and cute little pots and jars marked 'Miracle-working', and Dora's daily suggestions that I Do Something with my hair.

Squashed on the deck between two old ladies and a trussed turkey I see again that strange, shaggy woman peering out furtively from the long mirror like a Thurber Animal surprised. It is a year since I have seen myself in a full-length mirror. I realise that another of life's milestones has been passed. I have Let Myself Go.

5

'George!' Creon approached with a rapid businesslike trot. He wore a white linen suit with a pink carnation, his reading glasses, and his official frown. 'We shall adjourn at once to Soteris' coffee house. I have a matter of serious nature to discuss with you.'

'Permits!' I groaned.

'No, no, no!' Creon said crossly. 'How many times am I to tell you that you are not to worry about this matter? Am I not your friend? No, no, no. This affair concerns that young French fellow.'

'Jacques?'

'Yes.' He nodded sternly. 'Here inside, where we will not be overheard.' We settled ourselves like conspirators at a marble-topped table against the side wall where we would not be seen from the street, and ordered our coffees. Creon sat stiffly and in silence, drumming his fingers on the table until the coffee was brought, then cleared his throat.

'My dear George,' he said, and folded his hands together, 'I have been approached this morning by a deputation of citizens, who come to me, not only because I am a leading citizen of the town, but also because I am your friend, and you happen to know this young Frenchman well. They wish to be fair in this matter and to give the young man warning.'

'What has he done now?' asked George, but at this very moment in the aching-bright oblong of the window Jacques himself shuffled slowly past against a background of ships' rigging and blue-and-white striped awnings. He wore very brief shorts and a ragged pink shirt arranged carelessly to expose completely one bare brown shoulder and his thickly curled chest. His golden head was bent to the matching spray of pink oleander that he carried delicately between two fingers. There was a dreamy smile touching his mouth. The gold earring glittered. At his side, and apparently oblivious to the fact that she towered a full head and shoulders over him, was the tall, curly headed Austrian girl who had been limpeting with him these last two days. Her hand also clasped a spray of pink oleander, and her pretty face had a blind, trance-like expression, which may have been due to the fact that her feet, which up to this time had been shod with sensible walking shoes, were quite bare, and lifting rather gingerly on the burning hot cobbles. A curious hush fell upon the crowded café tables until the pair had passed.

'*There*, George!' said Creon triumphantly, and gulped down his coffee. 'Mark you, I have no complaint to make personally. You and I are men of the world, after all. We have been young ourselves. I told the deputation they were old fools, of course, and gave them a short discourse on existentialism.'

'Yes, but what is the complaint, Creon?' asked George, looking like a man trying to digest the thought of Creon giving a lecture on existentialism.

'Why, you just saw him go past. You have eyes! Mothers are keeping their daughters locked up inside the houses now at the hour of *peripató*.'

'You mean he's accused of seducing the village girls?'

'I mean nothing of the sort. But the parents of the girls think it not nice for young and modest girls to see him with his shirt undone like that, and his feet with no shoes on all over the café table. I deplore his manners, but I still think they are a lot of old fools. I told them so, George. I told them so. But they demand that he button up his shirts and puts his shoes on and behaves himself in public, or they will go to the police and ask for his removal from the island.'

George promised that he would pass on the complaint.

'He'll only make that loud blurting noise he makes whenever he thinks of banality,' I said.

George shrugged.

Even in the unlikely event that Jacques *did* do up his buttons and put sandals on, the good citizens would not sleep quiet. They are outraged, and very properly. They would be outraged even if he draped himself from head to foot in sackcloth. For there *is* something totally outrageous about him. So the citizens of Thebes locked up their daughters when Dionysos entered their city with his following of barefooted Oriental women who were no Greeks but 'sang for joy in foreign tune ...'

'There's brute wildness in that jasmine flower,' sighed George, paraphrasing as wearily as Sean. 'Reverence it well.'

But the citizens are right. You just cannot have your daughters taking their shoes off. It's disruptive. It's against the common good. Banish him by all means. Everyone ought to assist. You can't have that walking around *loose*, as it were, without a chain and muzzle. God knows what might not happen! Just think what *did* happen in Thebes once the girls got the idea of taking off their shoes and running around the mountains!

''Ullo,' Jacques said unhappily. 'Am I going to be expelled again?'

'Why, have you been expelled before, Jacques?'

'Oh yes. Of course. From Iviza and Ischia and Capri and Corsica. And once, on Majorca, I was pelted with tomatoes.' He smiled a slow brave martyr's smile and carefully crossed his feet on the plastic tablecloth.

6

So the mountains simmer and melt and harden again at evening. That curling bronze crest never breaks quite, and at night the white houses sleep under it in seeming peace, but strange, Oriental, a Tibetan monastery perhaps, peaceful about the navel of navels, the mystery of mysteries. The cats howl, the donkeys hoot and honk, the owl's liquid notes are lost in a rasp of music from a near *taverna* where the dispossessed in blue jeans are dancing out their secret sorrows.

Somewhere on the waterfront Sean is yawning, thinking of the words, all the words yet to be strung together before the novel is finished, Lola is all for going on somewhere else. Black John and Dora are sitting in the Poison Pit, half-amused and half-horrified at the spectacle of drunken Feodor hammering nails into his thigh with the flat of his palm, Creon is making hot milk for Zoë and developing to her his short lecture on existentialism, and in the bottom floor of the little white house rented by Dionysos of the St-Germain-des-Pres the good woman who has retired early to bed is awakened yet again by the wheezing, Bacchic strains of 'Par Epano' and a cascade of wine jetting through the ceiling.

The nights are velvet. We have moved our mattresses and the children's up to the top-floor terrace, and there, under the great purple night all prodigal with stars, we sleep, or do not sleep, wish on each meteor trailing light across the sky, lean on the parapet watching the dark sea, the pale houses, smoke endless cigarettes, talk in whispers, listen to the snores and restless turnings and stirrings and murmurs from other terraces where other human beings are lying on their mattresses sleeping or not sleeping under the stars.

How sweetly the children sleep with thin, naked brown arms flung wide and sun-bleached heads gleaming silver in the starlight. Already they have almost forgotten that there was another life before this, when they did not breakfast by the sea, when they did not sleep under the sky. Looking at them sweetly sleeping one has a little unreasonable stirring of faith again. Through them we are committed wholly to life: the enterprise is sound. One can work a little longer, try a little harder. Nothing yet was ever accomplished by resignation or despair, no set of circumstances was ever bettered by the willingness to put up with it, or submit to it. Against all reason I find myself sneaking a sight on another of those staging posts of mine. When the new manuscripts are finished ...

'It's too hot to sleep,' says George. 'Let's go and swim.'

Together we tiptoe out of the dark house, through the lanes where the cats stalk, along the sleeping waterfront, and take the cliff path until we come to the fig-tree. Silently we descend to the dark water, silently leave our pale, crumpled heap of clothes, silently slip into the wet black silk where the briny stars wake at a movement and catch and cling and stream slow trails from our nakedness, from breast and foot and fingertip that move again with wonder and delight, made marvellous by the night and the sea.

August

I

Day by day the heat increases, and day by day the ships — for the *Sirina* is reinforced now by a second steamer — unload their quotas of family holiday parties from Athens, tourists from everywhere, and artists for the School. Socrates is mad with business, and even old Stamatis has finally abandoned his sinkers and sits mute and unprotesting outside Maria's shop, crowned ludicrously with a fringed cone of acid-yellow straw from the rainbow pile of comic hats which Maria is dispensing to stout Athenian ladies.

The waterfront is a sea of coffee tables, bobbing gaily with young women in tight pants and young men in beards and tight pants, and interesting-looking people of uncertain age and sex who wear their hair smartly jagged and carry artists' portfolios. A babble of foreign tongues rises and explodes in shrieks of laughter.

In the little jewel-green scoop of harbour there are yachts at anchor now, sleek, beautiful, expensive toys with tall masts from which droop the still, bright folds of the flags of Italy, of France, of Panama, of the U.S.A. Our sunbathing ledges are spread now with flesh in every degree of suntan and comeliness, and the triangle of water fenced in by the shark net is aswarm with aquatic monsters, goggle-eyed, rubber-snouted, and balancing ping-pong balls on the curved and corrugated antennae of their snorkels.

Jacques is appearing unshaved, dark about the eyes, and surly with tiredness, too exhausted to even be triumphant that he has answered the complaint of the good citizens by organising whole troops of young men and women (foreign and Athenian) who go up and down the waterfront at promenade time wearing only the briefest shorts, with unbuttoned shirts, and their feet all bare. The Bacchae are everywhere, and the revels are night long.

It is obvious now that Creon was wrong in dismissing the transient bohemians as unimportant. Maria's instinct was much more sound. One should have known even from the advent of the blue-jeaned nomads, whose noses are infallible for the smelling out of the smart place. One should have guessed what was happening from the number of houses reconditioned or in process of reconditioning, from the bright new paint on the waterfront shops and the café blackboards laboriously printed out in misspelt English and French as well as Greek, from the numbers of people — foreign as well as Athenian — who have been making inquiries about the possibility of purchasing houses.

For now it is apparent that the yearly passage of the smart, penniless, immoral, clever young people — Creon's 'bums and perverts' — has had its inevitable effect. This beautiful little port is to suffer the fate of so many beautiful little Mediterranean ports 'discovered' by the creative poor. Here, where the merchant princes lived like feudal lords, where legends and heroes were bred, and where at last the great houses sank down into the stones, is happening the last renaissance, the last sad renaissance of all. After the artists come the people with the leisure and the money and the taste to be amused by artists, and the people with big yachts and big bank accounts who send the cost of living so high that the poor artists are forced to move on and discover another little port. We are watching the island in the process of becoming *chic*.

'Are you liking it more now, Katharine?' I asked, meeting her early by the market stalls.

'Oh, it's so ghastly I could die! Toby and I are just hiding away and praying there'll be an earthquake or something to send these awful people packing. I don't know why people just can't leave us *alone*!' she added aggrievedly, evidently feeling that the tourists are a personal affront. 'And now, on top of everything, my mother has decided to drop by for a visit.'

'Won't that be nice?'

'Oh,' said Katharine bleakly.

2

Katharine's mother has arrived, a short, stout, formidable woman of healthy middle age, with round, black, inquisitive eyes and the high, precise voice of one accustomed to addressing committee meetings.

She has declined to stay with Katharine and Toby, and instead has rented the top floor of Little Cuckoo's house, which is just around the corner from us. She is prepared to stay for a month or two, believing, I gather, that Katharine must come to her senses in that time and persuade Toby to return to America and take a university post. If Katharine fails to come to her senses Mrs Knip looks quite capable of abandoning her to her fate. In the meantime she is prepared to civilise the island.

She appears on the waterfront at precisely eleven-thirty each morning in something of the manner of an anthropologist or lady missionary, tightly corseted under her best dress of uncrushable nylon, wearing a large straw hat, new *espadrilles*, and carrying a Japanese parasol. The villagers are very properly terrified of her, for although she has not a single word of Greek she manages to convey her meaning quite distinctly.

Little Cuckoo, herself an inquisitive woman, was startled out of her wits the other morning when she crept up the back stairs while Mrs Knip was out — 'just to see what the Kyria was cooking for lunch' — to find a bucket of water balanced on the trap door in such a way that another incautious step would have brought the contents down on Little Cuckoo's head. Neighbouring ladies who have dropped by in their friendly, curious, chattering way before the Kyria was out of bed, have found themselves being ushered to the door by a fleshy shimmer of nylon nightgown, where the Kyria has given them a short demonstration of the use of the doorknocker. Before that bright black eye they all quail.

Evidently working on the principle that it is best to start civilising those immediately around her, Mrs Knip on her second morning here demanded from Little Cuckoo a large apron, a big bowl, hot water, and a full parade of Little Cuckoo's children. The children were all lined up and Mrs Knip proceeded to bathe them all thoroughly with strong green soap and disinfectant. The children were too terrified to run away or even do more in way of protest than to snivel hopelessly. Now, every morning when she is dressed to go out, she appears regally on the balcony, calls down to Little Cuckoo, and makes vigorous washing motions. Terrified, Little Cuckoo gets out the tubs, lines up the children. Once satisfied that the ablutions are properly under way, Mrs Knip raises her parasol and sets out for the waterfront.

At the quay she sits in a canvas chair under the awning outside Panyotes' coffee house, with a straw swatter on a handle beside her to deal with the wasps, a glass of fresh lemon juice in front of her, and a pile of postcards and envelopes. From this vantage point she observes the life of the port from out of those round, black, inquisitive eyes set deep in her pudgy snub-nosed face.

She is like a squat black pistol pointed at all the vagueness, the summer indolence, the moral laxity of the foreign colony. Nobody escapes her.

'Come and sit down, young man, and tell me what *you* do.'

'Why, I paint, Mrs Knip.'

'You do? How nice. There seem to be so many artists here. And where do you exhibit?'

'Well, actually I've never exhibited yet.'

'Oh, painting is your hobby then. But what do you *do*?'

Rather uncomfortably, the young man explains that he travels a lot. His source of income is immediately extracted from him, the amount of his monthly remittance, his family name, his background. Implacably Mrs Knip delves to expose every shabby little secret. Of no use now for him to quote Racine. Mrs Knip has never heard of Racine.

'Well,' she will say at last, having exposed the last shame, the final horror, 'you *are* getting on, you know, aren't you now? You must decide whether you are to continue in this way. It's understandable for a boy to want to see the world, but then you aren't a boy any more, are you? And you've seen it all anyway, you tell me. Why, at your age my John is the father of a fine growing family and vice-president of two corporations. Besides,' she adds implacably, 'this life is obviously bad for your digestion. You've a terrible colour for such a young man. Are you constipated?'

Kierkegaard has nothing to answer and slinks away.

The intellectual hoboes are avoiding Mrs Knip like the very plague. She humiliates them too much. Only Sykes clings to her, wallowing in an orgy of confession; and Feodor, doing a mad-genius act that horrifies and fascinates her. Really, deeply, all Europeans horrify her.

'And what do *you* do, young man?' she demanded of Jacques one morning, having cornered him in the next canvas chair.

'Make love,' Jacques murmured sleepily in his best Yves Montand voice, and undid another button.

Mrs Knip has given it out as her considered opinion that Jacques is *dangerous*.

Toby and Katharine, with very wan, set faces, are acting as Mrs Knip's guides. Through the burning early afternoon heat they make excursions ... by mule to the monastery of the Prophet Elias, by motor launch to the further bays and hamlets, by foot to the great houses. No part of the island is left unexplored. With her parasol aloft Mrs Knip is everywhere — even at night to the taverns, where she grimly watches the young island men dancing.

'Dancing! That is not dancing, Katharine! Wiggling about like that! They ought to be ashamed of themselves, such strong-looking young men. Why don't you get out there and show them, Katharine.'

'Oh, *Mother*!' Katharine cries expiringly, in shame.

'But you learnt folk dancing for ten years, dear. What is the use of learning a thing if you have no intention of using it? You and Toby ought to be out there, singing and dancing, a pair of young people like you. Young people ought to be happy. Are you not happy, Katharine?'

'Oh, *Mother*, for heaven's sake —'

'I don't know why you're here then, if you aren't happy about it. Is she constipated, Toby? Make her drink more herb tea. She always did need a little help even when she was a girl. Mr Stavris assured me that the mountain herbs here are very efficacious. I *believe* in herbs. For the blood, particularly.'

For Creon she has a very high regard. He is a man of dignity and sense. Together they plan cottage hospitals and yacht clubs, convert the House of Usher into a tourist hotel, turn the old market into a cinema.

Creon has not been so happy since I have known him. His America is hers — an America of shrewd business dealings, hard work, admirable returns, progress, prosperity, and efficient sanitation. And neither of them understands why all these young men should not have been satisfied amid such a plethora of plenty and opportunity.

'As I see it, Mr Stavris,' says Mrs Knip, 'art is for artists. It has no value whatsoever in the course of ordinary human affairs except as a relaxation for people of sufficient means to enjoy it. I do not decry it, of course. I have seen every museum in Europe, Mr Stavris, in the course of the last year. Every museum. Katharine will tell you that I am nothing if not thorough. And in spite of seeing every museum and monument of antiquity I don't mind telling you that sometimes I have had time on my hands, time to fill in. Then how can these young men spend their lives at it? Either they don't do it thoroughly, Mr Stavris, or else they're shamming. And I suspect that they *are* shamming.'

'Bums and perverts, madam! Hoboes!' And Creon, dapperly suited in white linen, blows his nose with a dismissive blast on a beautifully laundered handkerchief.

'No, Mr Stavris. Misdirection. They're really good clean American young men who have been misdirected. They think they ought to admire Europe because they have been told that Europe is admirable. So they try to become Europeans instead of good Americans. The leopard cannot change his spots, Mr Stavris. You can see how bad it is for them. Is there one of these young men who is genuinely happy being a European? No. They're unhappy, Mr Stavris, and unhappy because in their hearts they despise Europe. Being Americans they have energy, and no way of using it, and that is why they go round and round so much. My! All that good American energy going round and round wastefully, churning and churning. It's no wonder they take to drugs and debauchery.'

'No wonder at all, Mrs Knip.'

'Admiring art doesn't use up their energy, Mr Stavris. Because they don't admire it really. No American does, except in its proper place. They only think they *ought to*. Now, if any one of them had the courage to admit his error and go back home again, why he'd be a happy man again. All that experience he could sell. Foreign languages, foreign food, art, architecture, furniture ... limitless opportunities to use his energy and none of his experience need be wasted. Because they're all very clever, you know. Just listen to their accents. You'd never know Sykes Horowitz was born in the Bronx, would you? And the way he rattles on with French, it's a treat to listen to.'

Every evening she holds court — judicial rather than regal on the waterfront by the Poison Pit. There are three tables pushed together. Drawn by the terrible and inexorable magnetism of Mrs Knip, the entire foreign colony eats and drinks communally.

'Katharine's cooking was never her strong point, and that house of hers is so *stuffy*. Of course, how any woman can hope to cook any edible food on those smelly little burners is just beyond me. No wonder Greek food is so bad. I just have that young man do a charcoal-broiled steak for me, and I mix the dressing for the salad myself. Why do they have no tarragon here? Sykes, you ought to do the same as I. How do you expect your digestive system to function if you keep on with those terrible stuffed tomatoes? Why, I can hear you rumbling from this distance!'

Sean murmurs *sotto voce*, 'Better a handful with quietness than two handfuls with labour and a striving after wind.'

Someone sniggers. Katharine and Toby sit on either side of Mrs Knip, suffering exquisitely at being publicly identified as

155

part of a Foreign Group. For Mrs Knip has made a jolly social club and she intends that membership be constant.

George drags me along the waterfront at breakneck pace, pretending to point out something further along the quay, but it seldom works. Mrs Knip has the eye of an eagle.

Even the cave has ceased to be our refuge at night. Mrs Knip arranges picnic parties there, with community singing. She believes in communal activities; they keep young people out of mischief. At the same time, she is genuinely curious about everything and everybody and anxious for people to be happy. She is organising caiques for trips around the island and across to the mainland; somewhat to their own surprise the decadents are finding themselves planning picnic lunches and telling Mrs Knip about their childhoods in Wisconsin and Brooklyn and even Iowa, and playing rounds of table tennis in Johnny Lulu's coffee house.

'There,' says Mrs Knip with evangelical satisfaction, 'I don't know why God bothered making the world if nobody is to be pleased about it. People were meant to be happy. I am constantly pointing out to Katharine that to have had an unhappy life is to have been a failure. What's the matter, Katharine? You look quite ill. You aren't pregnant, are you?'

'*Mother*, I will …'

But what Katharine will do we are not to know, for she jumps up from the communal table and rushes down along the quay, quite distraught. Toby hurries after her.

'I don't wonder that the child is becoming hysterical,' says Mrs. Knip forbearingly. 'Living like a peasant the way she does. After the education and opportunities that girl has had. Well, well, perhaps she will come to her senses yet.'

3

And day by day the heat increases. It is hot when we get up at five in the morning. In the midday hours it is quite impossible to move outside. The light leaps back from reflecting white planes in searing sheets. Your eyes wince and blink and fill with water to even look up at the mountains. At midnight the cobbles are still warm.

The white house walls that look so cool and pale in the moonlight have a dry, hot, plastery feel which is curiously unpleasant. The sun is sealed into stone and street and wall and rock. In the dark the whole town shimmers on the parched black mountains like a scattered pile of bleached bones.

We thirst all the time for grapes and melons and peaches, for handfuls of ice, for water in frosted glasses, and live on little else but fruits and salads. Cooked food is revolting, the very sight and smell of olive oil is enough to turn the stomach. The dog lies panting on the stone floor of the kitchen, covered with clusters of ticks like squelchy bunches of grapes; George does all he can to remove them but the animal has become an obscenity. There is a plague of wasps. From the garden comes a constant low-pitched humming; there are wasps crawling in the sugar bowl, wasps drowned in glasses of water, wasps caught in the sweaty strands of one's hair. They have stripped all the grapes from the vine, which is now hung with festoons of flaccid, juiceless skins. I am only glad that we bought the icebox before the royalty statements came in. Cold food and cold showers keep us alive.

George has to go for the ice the moment he is out of bed. The ice factory is as inadequate as the town's electricity plant, and every morning the crowd gathers at dawn, three hundred people who know full well that there will be no more than a hundred half-blocks of ice for distribution.

When Costas opens the doors everyone surges forward, and the weaker men and all the women and children are trampled under or swept aside. Costas solves the problem by simply taking the half-blocks and heaving them through the door until they are all gone. I suppose the system is as effective as any. George gets a block three times out of five, but then he is very tall and in his youth took part in a football scrum every Saturday afternoon. He comes home from the ice scrum panting and excited, dragging the prize behind him on a length of frayed rope, and attacks the pump with an astonishing vigour, doing a Walter Mitty in the mirror opposite.

In the immediate neighbourhood ours is the only icebox and all day long little children come with jugs to be filled with ice-water from our tank. We fill them while we can in the cause of neighbourliness, but feel cross nevertheless. The tank is always drained when we need ice-water ourselves. Besides, most of the water now has to be brought by Elias from the Sweet Wells, and the cost of buying it is getting alarming.

One is becoming worried also about the level in the storage cistern under the floor. Perhaps it is not as capacious as Socrates had indicated. And of what use our shower room and sanitary toilet arrangements if there is no water to pump into the tank? Cassandra still refuses to use water from the well outside for domestic purposes on the grounds that it is brackish, full of minerals, and too heavy. Uncharitably I suspect that she is enchanted with water running from a tap and feels she might lose caste by going out with a bucket and rope like the other women.

For the time being we are continuing to take showers every day — a luxury that consoles us for other shortcomings — and the toilets still whoosh away in a grand crescendo. It must be the queerest sound in an island night. All the lanes of the town are pervaded by a stench that rises above the jasmine and gardenias. Obviously everybody else is feeling the want of water too.

For the Feast of the Virgin Mary, on the fifteenth of August, thousands of pilgrims come to the island. There is no accommodation left. They sleep the night in the courtyard of the monastery, under the patch of pines on the cliff above the cave, and even around the cave itself, with blankets and foodstuffs spread out on the ledges.

And after the *Panaygia* and the pilgrims comes the *meltémi*.

Now the air begins to whine and shriek as burning blasts of wind gust and rip through the smelly lanes, churning old newspaper, ice-cream wrappings, dried donkey droppings, tourists' litter, and clouds of powdered white plaster that has been flaked from parched walls. Loose shutters and heat-warped doors bang and crash, tiles lift, whole panes of glass blow out from windows. In the garden the leaves curl and shrivel on the citrus trees, plants droop limply, and there is no water to spare for them.

One's hair is wisped and tangled, one's skin covered with a layer of powdered plaster that turns to paste with the sweat and makes a weird clown's mask.

In spite of the heat we must bring our beds down from the terrace, for the wind whips all the sheets away in the night, and one cannot sleep under the rain of plaster, old newspapers, and even flying roof tiles.

But how the sea changes and lives with a life of its own! The yachts are leaping at their anchorage. The milky gulf is turned capricious, mood indigo now with Poseidon's wild blue horses leaping and fretting and tossing their manes of streaming white. The cave is Cavern Perilous. Here the water lifts in transparent viridian peaks that hurl right over the platforms, here it rushes running and sucking down the spiny shelf where the sea urchins cling, here it churns into thick yellow froth like whipped cream. There is a mad exhilaration in swimming in such wild water. You are flung high, buffeted, lifted, tossed. Now you are fighting up through foam, with bursting lungs and aching limbs: now above you a transparent peak hummocks and lifts a waving white body like a strange, soft starfish caught in the sunmesh: now it is yourself hurled high ... and now, now, for a delirious second, the power rears beneath you, your hair is streaming in the streaming mane, and gloriously you are riding the wild wild horse of Poseidon.

Confined to the secondary excitements of dodging the waves crashing over the ledges, the children beg to be allowed to swim. Almost I say yes, for they are strong swimmers and love the sea's society as I do. I hate to deprive them of this most marvellous experience. Yet it is undeniably dangerous in the water, and incredibly difficult to get out, for unless you judge the moment when a wave breaks high on the ladder you are likely to be scraped down the rock among the sea urchins or sucked into a yellow ice-cream churn of foam where it is impossible to breathe. Two swimmers have been very close to drowning within the last couple of days, and now there are only half a dozen of us, led by Lola (who swims like a seal), still going in every day. The iron net is split wide, the drums have been wrenched loose and half of them are tossing down the gulf or washed up on rocks miles away. On the quay a caique unloads the drowned body of a young man wreathed in wet brown weed.

'Mummy, he was *smelling!*' Shane draws out the word thrillingly, horrifically, her hand making exclamatory circles, her blue eyes wide and shining. But now both children watch warily from the ledges while we swim, and buffet us with assumed negligence when we are safely out again.

The smell stays with me too, in my nostrils and the back of my throat, the oozy, sweetish, briny smell of black sponges dying, of rotting shellfish, of stranded weed aswarm with flies. Sometimes, for a mad moment, when my hand slips on the ladder and the iron rungs suddenly leap feet above my head and the weeds pour down, or I feel myself being hurled forward towards those jagged, streaming rocks, the smell rises as though my mouth was stuffed with oozy sponges, and I am filled with something that is terror and desire both ... to ride on with the wild wild horses to the waiting cliff, or to curl up small, close against the scaly rocks, to curl up small and let the wild horses ride over me.

4

But everyone is gone a little mad now. Perhaps it is only that the heat and the *meltémi* affect the emotional climate. Perhaps an artificial atmosphere is created by these hordes of sophisticated people superimposed upon a simple island pattern that has no place or provision for them. Artificial or not, the atmosphere seems bad, sick somehow, and it permeates the whole town.

Feodor slit his own belly with a knife in the Poison Pit, another of his periodic 'suicides', and staggered along the quay all bedabbled with blood. I know the port has seen worse things than this in its roaring days, but things of violence and passion that rose inevitably from a reckless, expansive way of life. Feodor's public exhibitionism only seems boring and dirty, and all the messier since someone has to clean up after him. And then he goes on operating on cats. His hands and clothes are often covered with gangrenous matter that he never bothers to wash off; he smells so strongly of corruption and decay that when he scratches himself one almost expects to see the flesh adhere to his fingers.

'It is difficult to believe,' said George carefully, 'that somewhere inside that carcase lies the unquenchable spirit — God, if you like!... The light that has never flickered out since the first stirring of the protoplasm ... all that way to ... to Feodor.' He shuddered, and taking one of his Tibetan prayer wheels down from the wall, began to spin it slowly. '*Om Mane Padme Hum*,' he intoned, and then, blanching at the sudden thought: 'My God! Suppose Feodor *is* the Jewel in the Lotus!'

George is a little mad too. So is Sean, who has taken to singing the Liffey passages from *Finnegan's Wake* at a certain stage in his cups, to the same tuneless chant that he uses for 'Ophelia's Song', Blake's 'Sick Rose', and 'I'll Take You Home Again, Kathleen'. In between going to parties and nagging at Sean, Lola picks all the skin off her feet, or sits among the ruins, intently studying rubbish dumps, which she says she is going to paint from the observation point of an ant.

Explosions occur. There are tavern brawls, scratchy quarrels around tables on the waterfront, parties in yachts and houses that culminate in a currently popular game called 'Sardines' — a sad, lewd sniggery echo of those boisterous Games of Gargantua called Trudge-pig, Twirly Whirlytril, and Prickle Me Tickle Me, which my father used to read out with tears streaming down his cheeks and both hands clasped over his shaking belly ... how long ago?

While the *poste-restante* boys are playing 'Sardines' with yachting parties and bright young things, Jacques has abandoned charm and turned apache. Now when he is not wooing he snarls at the villagers and spoils for a fight with the labourers who frequent the same *tavernas*. Only when Katharine is of the company does he revert to tawny tomcat, and purr sleepily in his soft, slow voice, or lightly, with insinuation, brush against her in passing. Softly, deliberately, a step at a time, he is stalking her, and stalking her publicly. Katharine's blue eyes are wide with surprise and terror, but her hands are shaking and her voice is quick and nervous instead of sighing. Sometimes she blazes into astonishing prettiness, particularly since she has left off wearing that dreary headscarf. Toby has become angry, uncertain, over-possessive with Katharine in public — over-ready, too, to quarrel with Mrs Knip, who is watching it all from her bright black eyes.

'I have come to the conclusion that this is a *de*-moralising place and a *de*-moralising way of life.' Mrs Knip offered her conclusion to the gathering outside the Poison Pit in her best committee-meeting voice, like a president officiating at the winding-up of a company. 'It is not my business to interfere, Toby, but if you and Katharine want to eat lotus I suggest that the only place you are likely to find any is right back home.'

Toby snorted angrily. 'Yes, I know. Only the tenderest buds, deep-frozen, in goddam p-p-plastic packs and ten different mouth-watering flavours!'

'Can't you understand, Mother,' Katharine cried, 'that we don't *want* all that? That we hate it, and won't belong to it? That we mean to live our own lives in truth and simplicity, free from all that terrible slavery to machines and gadgets? That we *must* find our own paths?'

'Mind you don't stumble then, miss,' said Mrs Knip slyly, and Katharine flamed scarlet, Toby compressed his mouth under the huge Greek moustache, and Jacques lowered his heavy eyelids and began to whistle 'Par Epano' very softly through his teeth.

But there are times when I begin to think that Mrs Knip is right. The atmosphere *is* bad. And I wonder if Feodor's operations are worse, in fact, than the spectacle of angelic little Aphrodite and Persephone crouched together in a lane quite absorbed in dropping stones on a batch of newborn kittens.

Everything is changed, as though I am looking at the island in a distorting mirror, or as if the moon has begun to shine on us with her other face.

The old woman sweeping the church doorstep looks up at me as I pass, and her eyes are white with trachoma. Two adolescent louts are teasing the dwarf girl and she is laughing — why did I never notice before that she has two sets of teeth? All the Bosch people have crawled out from their dark corners and are limping and hopping and gibbering in the sweltering sun: the face in the window has a beak like a parrot, the baby dead of malnutrition is a swollen toad, a woman shrieks among the windburnt geraniums with the howling mouth of a Greek mask — gone mad, they say, with waiting for her man to return from the sea — the hand that measures out a mound of glistening green grapes is not a hand at all, but a sort of double-hooked claw covered with scabs. Eyes are furtive, mouths are leering, bodies are swollen and misshapen. On the butcher's slab a skinned bull's head all covered with flies slides slowly towards me in a mess of slippery scarlet. Four boys with poles and hooks are fishing cruelly for birds on the hill above the Down School. The flyblown carcase of a dead cat is rotting in Kyria Spirathoula's hen run, and every lane and rooftop and alley is aswarm with live ones — huge, slinking, predatory and lust-haunted brutes all torn and mangy and scarred. In a dark archway a young sailor snickers and his old companion, dressed expensively in yachting clothes, lurches back into the shadows ...

I cannot seem to blink back into focus. The tiers of ruins seem more real than the gay and crowded waterfront. The island died long long ago; the antics of all the smart bright people who throng the café tables suddenly have the ultimate obscenity of necrophilia.

'Now I wonder if you would give me a little assistance,' said Mrs Knip, visiting again to use our shower and wash out her nylons. 'I think a committee of residents must be organised to deal with the increasing menace of *these cats*. Now, if we had a dozen people divided into six scouting parties of two, and each party managed to catch six cats every night, in two or three weeks we could effect a considerable decrease in the numbers of cats. Each party would be provided with a sack, a pair of leather or rubber gloves, and the necessary chloroform and cotton wool. We would be doing the community a real service.'

'I think you'll find it dangerous work, trying to catch those monsters, Mrs Knip.'

'Dangerous? It's certainly more dangerous to allow them to prowl around! I have discovered that it is the practice here to kill off practically all female kittens at birth. Those alley cats are therefore frustrated males, and it is my belief that no woman is safe with them. Would you be kind enough, George, to pump a little more water? This tap is not running.'

But the pump only made anguished sucking noises, and the beam of a flashlight shone down into the black shaft of the cistern revealed the pipe inlet dry above an expanse of mud from which protruded a rusty can, three clothes pegs, and the sandal Shane had sworn she left in Rita's house.

Bundling her unrinsed nylons into a plastic bag, Mrs Knip was very thoughtful. 'That's too bad,' she said, intimating that she would take them round to Katharine's house and rinse them in well water.

'I wouldn't have troubled you at all this morning, but I do try not to interfere with Katharine and Toby. They must work out their own problems. I must say I am thankful that things seem to be coming to a head at last. Katharine is quite hysterical, you know, and she has taken to going off all morning by herself.' Mrs Knip looked slyly pleased. 'If Toby is any sort of man he won't stand *that* for long. He will surely see that this place is *de*-moralising.'

Yet she did not go, but watched with interest — with anthropological interest perhaps — while George and I scrambled down the dank, hollow shaft of the cistern to see for ourselves its extent and what repairs and cleaning would be necessary before the winter rains. Standing in the black slime fifteen feet below the kitchen floor I felt Mrs Knip's hands capable and firm on the other end of the rope knotted under my shoulders, and her voice came echoing weirdly down the shaft as she chattered indefatigably on. The huge black cavern was curiously warm.

'You must not think that I don't admire the way you all *manage* in these terrible circumstances. Gracious me, every one of you deserves a medal, and it is only surprising to me that poor Katharine has put up with it all for as long as she has. Toby, you know, could command a very important position in one of our universities, and I am sure he will do so once the two of them have come to their senses. And then there is that nice Mr Donovan and his wife, such charming, intelligent people, living like rats in an attic — rats in an attic — when he might be playing an honourable role in shaping the minds of future generations.'

'Shit!' said George briefly as he dropped the flashlight into the mud and plunged us both into impenetrable blackness. Mrs Knip's pudgy face appeared in the circle of the shaft, high high above us, very small and distinct as seen through the wrong end of a telescope. Her voice came down in a series of reverberating pings that followed each other in a rising inflexion of wonder:

'But what I want to know is what are you doing it *for*?'

5

The combination of heat, waterlessness, the decadents, and Mrs Knip is working badly on George.

He broods about them in the sweaty windblown watches of the night, and threatens to sell the house and go back to London. From being a gregarious, warm-hearted, talkative, generous, and romantic fellow he has become suspicious, moody, unfriendly, irritable, and despairing. His work too is causing him concern. Nothing seems to go right with it, although he works harder than ever, patiently exploring every avenue, every corridor of possibility that might lead to some sort of security … or is it an escape now that he is working for?

It has become an obsession with both of us to try to avoid that tainted arena of the waterfront with its traps of tables and wine flasks, where still the shafts of spite and envy and malice break and splinter, and still under the loops of naked bulbs the dislocated psyches creak and crack, the obscure philosophers are trotted out, the negligent poems never completed, the revolutionary paintings never begun, and the interminable verbal catch-ball with esoteric phrases about linear values and plastic form that inflame George to a white-heat of fury.

Linear values! He has just discovered the basic values of having enough food in the pot to keep alive two adults and three hungry children. And since it has come to him at a time in his life when he might reasonably have expected to have made adequate provision for such an elementary need, it has to him a shattering significance, like a revelation. He is become a furious prophet crying woe and damnation to anyone who is short-sighted or irresponsible enough to take it for granted.

The children are blissfully unaware of the significance of the cooking pot. Every day they shoot up as if they have been watered overnight. Beautiful, wild young things they are, and beautiful too the fat brown baby who laughs now and clutches handfuls of air and wonderingly discovers his own waving fingers. They weigh upon my heart like lead, like chains, like three strong anchors bedded deep in the reality from which I can never escape — not even into despair.

Oh, if only one could afford the luxury of one good wallow in despair, or the greater luxury of a moment's indolence, or even that final temptation to surrender to hysteria, like Katharine! (That one brief image apprehended before one could will it back into unrecognition, of her tall figure scrambling wildly up through the parched rocks and the spikes of asphodel near the cemetery, and Jacques leaning idly on a splintered wooden cross, tracing a name with one finger.)

And all the time in the frenzied daily round of cooking and cleaning and trying to maintain order, while the typewriter chatters along and the stoves explode or George staggers backwards and forwards from the well outside with buckets of water for the dying trees, Mrs Knip's clear, bright voice goes on pinging in my head:

'But what are you doing it *for*?'

6

Shopping in the *agora* very early this morning we encountered Jacques stumbling out of the pharmacy. His shirt was hanging in strips about his shoulders, and the lower half of his face was covered entirely with a black scarf. The visible half wore an expression of infinite suffering.

"Ullo,' he said, unhappily.

'Toothache?' George asked. 'Or are you playing pirates?'

'I 'ave a toothache,' Jacques said. 'I think I 'ave several toothaches.' He sat down suddenly and very heavily on the kerb and put his head between his knees. Anastasis and Tomas, two labourers who were trundling wicker-crated jars of acid up the quay with absorbed deliberation, exploded into sniggers as they passed. One of the EOKA youths walked by whistling 'Par Epano'.

'I think you'd better come with us and have a brandy,' George said. We got him propped up in a chair at the back of Katsikas' store, and Nicko, his face carefully non-committal, brought a big tumbler of brandy. Jacques drank it under the loose end of the black scarf, fumbling in a strange, nerveless sort of way.

'How did you come by your toothache?'

Jacques sighed and shook himself slightly. 'I think it was a shoe,' he said. 'I think I remember somebody's shoe in my face.'

'Where were you?'

'In a *taverna,* I suppose. On all the other nights I am in a *taverna*, so I suppose I was in a *taverna* last night. I 'ave the sort of 'eadache I get after being in a *taverna*.'

'But don't you know?'

'Could I 'ave another brandy, do you think?' Jacques asked with unnatural politeness. His voice was faint and far-away. There were little pinpoints of sweat springing all over the bit of his face you could see, and his eyes were swivelling strangely.

'If you are feeling sick we ought to get you something to eat.'

'No, thank you. It doesn't matter. I don't think I 'ave any teeth left to eat with.'

George made a funny little stifled grunt, and both my hands flew to my mouth.

'I 'aven't counted the ones in my pocket yet, but there seem to be a lot. I can remember spitting them out into my 'and.'

And suddenly I felt really, nauseatingly, sick myself. Those beautiful white teeth that had set hearts leaping at every flash of them, that had torn chunks of tough goat and stringy beef and cracked sunflower seeds and sunk into watermelons and peaches and God knows what other succulences besides.

The ghost of a smile twitched the black scarf in a curiously melancholy way. 'Oh, it's all right. I've 'ad all my teeth on screws for years. As long as I always remember to spit them out and put them in my pocket, it's not very 'ard for a dentist to screw them in again. Unaesthetical,' he added faintly, 'but practical.'

And as Mrs Knip entered the store at that moment and bore down on us in consternation we surrendered the suffering Jacques to her eminently practical ministrations. He caught the afternoon boat to Athens, leaving the village wild with speculation. Two of the Bacchae went with him, quite distraught with anxiety and in tears. Most people are agreed that this time he went too far, but as nobody knows for certain what happened, nobody can really say in what direction he has exceeded bounds. However, everyone agrees that it is scandalous.

I only know that tonight there was a group of labourers having some sort of celebration in Johnny Lulu's *taverna,* and that Toby, in passing, bought them an *oka* of wine.

7

The wine boats are going out. All the waterfront is ranked with oak barrels, washed and drying in the sun.

The smell of the resin is overpowering. The outgoing caiques are laden to their marks with barrels, and each barrel carries a sprig of bay leaves in the bung — it is curious and lovely, as though each caique had sprouted leaves from its planks.

Each day there is a little ceremony as a priest blesses each boat in turn as the empty barrels are loaded aboard, bidding it bring back good wine. The ritual, with its ancient implications, is somehow oddly reassuring.

Dionyssos is here, after all, and not in a dentist's chair in Athens. The old rhythm, the season's rhythm — of death, of resurrection, of growth, fruition, decay, and again resurrection —

waxes and wanes in its inexorable cycle; unaffected by the gentleman in Bermuda shorts and baseball cap who is trying, with light meter and expensive camera, to record the promise of joy implicit in those decks so anciently and beautifully murmurous with leaves.

For the first time in God knows how many weeks I want to sing; I want to take a mountain in each hand and clap them together like great brass cymbals; I want to find Mrs Knip all neat in her uncrushable nylons and drag her down the length of resin-reeking barrels.

'Look, Mrs Knip! Here is your answer. *This* is what we are doing it for!'

September

I

On the step of the old mill the fat little man in the baseball cap paused, chewed reflectively on his cigar, and said:

'Well, I guess we could knock a window in there and fix a false door here, and then there wouldn't be any call to change location for the mill sequence.'

'Yeah. Yeah.' His companion was an even smaller and fatter man, and he wore four cameras and a light meter as well as a baseball cap. 'Why don't you do that, Hank?' he said.

The Levantine-looking youth in the beautiful linen suit coughed and said deferentially: 'I am informed by the mayor that there *is* another mill, in perfect working order, on the mountain above the town.'

'Nope. No use. I'd need helicopters.'

'If you really need helicopters we'll get you helicopters.'

'Sure, I know you would. But we'll manage all right here. No great problems I can see. What we do is pull down that shack there and build up something real picturesque for the sequence where Montgomery first sees Lucasta on the balcony. We can make it real Greek ... a few columns, old statues — gimmicks like that.'

'Yeah. Why don't you do that, Hank?'

'Oh, I'll do it all right, boy. Sure, and we'll make the threshing floor right there where that crummy bandstand or what-have-you is now.'

'Excuse me, sir,' said the Levantine youth, 'but there *is* a threshing floor along further.'

'Sure, I saw it. No good, son. You got to realise we're going to need a threshing floor big enough to stack in a hundred and twenty-seven dancing girls as well as a *bouzouki* band and still leave room for the equipment. You always got to think of the equipment, son.'

'And you just wait till you see that equipment,' said the second little man proudly. 'Why, this little old island is going to be just loaded with equipment. Just loaded!'

'That's right,' said Hank, spitting out the brown end of his cigar. 'We'll take her apart. Yes sir! We're sure going to take this little old island apart,' he said with a hoarse chuckle.

To George and me, who had paused under the pine-trees on our way up from the cave to listen to this extraordinary conversation, this last remark seemed to hold an authentic oracular note.

The sun, huge and squashy crimson, was deflating slowly on the mountains of Arcady, and all the air was flushed with a last extravagant squandering of light. Salmon pink the sea and rose pink the mountains, and all the little islands taking on their evening colours of violet and pink and gold. A pink caique passed, laden with browny-pink goats. Level after level, tier upon tier, the white houses flushed rosy and a thousand panes of window glass dazzled suddenly gold.

The two fat little men slowly descended the steps of the old ruined mill, followed by the deferential Levantine youth.

'Why, sure,' the first little fat man said complacently, 'we'll take it apart all right. We sure will.'

2

Socrates bounded down the post office steps three at a time, wildly waving his straw sombrero. His fat little Turkish face was split with ecstasy.

'Ya! ya!' he yelled at us. 'Have you heard?'

'Heard what?'

He did a Chaplinesque pirouette among the crowded café tables and bounded through, shedding greetings to right and left as he came.

Plaintive cries followed him, from two family groups who, no doubt, were still waiting for accommodation.

'*Dollaria*, Kyrios Giorgios!' Socrates said breathlessly. 'Lots of *dollaria*!' He erupted into giggles, his hand making demented circles over his heaving belly. 'Oh, po-po-po-po! The Americans are coming here to make a moving picture, a big picture, and I am to find rooms for them. Eh? What do you think of that? A hundred and fifty rooms I have to find.'

'My God!' George and I looked at each other in horrified comprehension. So *that* was the reason for the two fat little men at the mill, and that hoarse, nasally voice prophesying dancing girls and *bouzouki* bands! 'We'll sure take this little old island apart! We sure will!'

'But what rooms, Socrates?' George asked with faint hope. 'Where do you think you can find a hundred and fifty rooms?'

'Pouf! I'll find them,' said Socrates gaily. 'All these houses. Look at them. Hundreds of houses! Up the mountain, down the mountain. I'll find rooms all right.' He laughed excitedly. '*Dollaria* for everyone, eh! Look at this cigar the Americanos gave me. He said you find me a hundred and fifty nice clean rooms with showers and —'

'*Showers!*' George stared at him. 'You've gone off your head, Socrates! There aren't any rooms with showers.'

'You've got a shower, haven't you?' Socrates countered accusingly. 'Kyrios Creon has a shower. Kyrios Georgaiki has a shower. Lots of places with showers.' His expansive gesture embraced the whole town.

'Socrates, don't talk such nonsense,' George said sternly. 'There aren't six houses on the island with showers, you know that. And none of those houses is for rent.'

Socrates clasped his hands over his belly and doubled up with laughter. '*Then pirasi!* Never mind, eh? Do you know what the Americanos said? He said Socrates you find me one nice clean house and it hasn't got a shower, I build one shower. *Dollaria,*

175

eh! That Americanos he has more *dollaria* than the king. Two million *dollaria* they're going to spend on this moving-picture, did you know that? Everyone's going to have a shower, going to have a lavatory with a chain, going to have lots of *dollaria* —'

'But Socrates, you bloody idiot, *there isn't any water*!'

'*Then pirasi!* God won't forget this island. He'll send a little bit of rain, you see. It's going to rain *dollaria* ...'

'*Dollaria!*' grinned Nicko Katsikas, cutting off fifty drams of the Cretan cheese with an unwonted extravagance and handing it across the counter with two glasses of the best *ouzo*. 'One of those Americanos bought my bottle of gin just now. I've had that bottle of gin on the shelf for five years. What do you think of that now? He said get plenty of gin, plenty of whiskey. Good health to us all! There are good times coming for everyone.'

'*Dollaria!*' Lefteri the house painter leaned over the table confidentially. '*Dollaria*, Kyrios Giorgios! Socrates says they want painters to fix up the waterfront real nice. You put in a good word for Lefteri, eh? I get some *dollaria*, maybe that bad woman of mine will come back and I can spit in her eye.'

'*Dollaria!*' Dinos the builder winked broadly and urged on the two small apprentices staggering along under hods of bricks. 'That Americanos wants the mill fixed up with sails on it, wants the threshing floor made out of concrete, wants little houses, wants new lampposts all along the waterfront. Maybe I'll buy that other storeyard from Tomas after all.'

'*Dollaria!*' said Tassos, said Giorgios, Spiros, Johnny Lulu, Andreas, Botzi, Panyotes, and even Dionyssos the dustman, adjusting the canvas dropping-bag under his donkey's tail.

'*Dollaria!*' said Tzimmy the pedlar, executing a mad little dance around his Benghazi basket.

*

'*Dollaria!*' hissed all the island wives, tucking up their skirts and getting out their buckets and sponges for a good clean out of their spare rooms.

But Friday, hurrying down the lane with white, incredulous face towards the house of Archonda the sempstress, tucked her pattern book and a new bolt of flowery cloth under her arm, spat three times, crossed herself with a terrible fervour, and said nothing at all.

3

Incredibly, it is happening. Like an invading army they are coming, with great weird landing barges that nose grimly into the tiny scoop of harbour and bear down on the moorings where the wine boats were blessed a week ago.

The dense, still clots of people on the quay sigh on a long exhaling note, and slowly, inexorably, the monstrous maws open and down the ramps roll the first wheels these cobbles have ever known — jeeps, trucks, trailers, tractors, half-tracks, strange, shrouded instruments, wheeled lamps. The ordnance of the conquering army.

From the lovely marble spire of the Monastery of the Virgin the great bronze bell crashes out the first stroke of noon, invoking a shattering roar of turning motors as the jeeps and vehicles move off in procession, a triumphal procession that is not the less impressively awful for being hampered by the inadequate length of the waterfront and the clutter of market stalls and café tables.

Now where the blue-ringed barrels were ranked are ranked thousands of crates and bales to be manhandled into the empty buildings taken over as warehouses. Teams of men in peaked caps and coveralls pelt up and down shouting inexplicable instructions. A small party of technicians, deliberate and concentrated among the gaping crowds of villagers and tourists, perform some esoteric rite with a theodolite and lengths of coloured string. Gangs of workmen recruited in the village swarm all over the waterfront buildings. Lefteri sits triumphant astride a swinging plank, a label pinned proudly to his shirt, sloshing lolly-pink limewash on to the pure white walls of an old house. Everywhere carpenters are hammering and sawing. Alongside the admiral and his marble lion a concrete mixer churns away in the middle of Panyotes' coffee tables. Like presidential candidates, two plump men in Hawaiian shirts and straw hats ride slowly in a jeep along the line of moored caiques, choosing those they will want repainted. On the steps of the post office an important personage in a peaked cap, followed deferentially by the Levantine youth, Socrates, and two blonde secretaries, barks briefly, 'Ruin that house!' and moves on.

The island is in a state of occupation.

4

And now, inevitably, there come the opportunists, the camp followers, the musicians and jugglers and sideshow barkers, the curious, the snobbish, the wealthy, the hopeful — all intent on participation. The harbour is so crammed with sleek yachts that there is scarcely room for the market caiques to come in. Speedboats buzz around the gulf like water beetles, towing young men and women on water-skis. The *Sirina* on every visit unloads hopeful young girls in job lots, standardised beauties with the currently favourite 'natural' look, who strike poses against ships' rigging or run gaily through the coffee tables with wide, white, animated smiles and superbly bouncing breasts.

We are introduced successively to Greece's champion diver, Greece's first violinist, Greece's most famous lyric poet, Greece's most brilliant young actress ... to dancers, singers, musicians, composers, writers, to photographers and photographers' models — all of whom have decided apparently that a late summer holiday on a quiet little island would be beneficial.

'Isn't all this *awful*!' they murmur in varying degrees of distaste, while absentmindedly smiling ecstatic smiles in the direction of the gentleman with two secretaries.

'Isn't this *awful!*' The culture group in patched blue jeans and stubbled chins shudder or sneer amusedly as inch by inch, accidentally, they hitch their chairs closer and closer to the table where a merry man in a Joseph coat is dispensing gin with a lavish pudgy hand on which a thick gold ring bites deeply into the little finger. Around his soft pink forearm, among the soft grey hair, a double row of gold links clasp an outsize watch, gold also. Everything of the most gorgeous. And at his side Creon, planked squarely in a café chair, frowning judicially, and smoking a cigar a foot long.

'Come right along, all you good folks! Come along now and help us out with this bottle. Say, you! Wotchername!' he calls happily over his shoulder to the Levantine youth, 'how about you rustle up some more gin from that store on the corner. I got guests. That's right. Move in now and forget your worries!'

Creon hitches up the knees of his beautifully darned and pressed pants, and brusquely flips five *drachmae* to the Levantine. 'Fetch peanuts, young man. And mind they are of the first quality.'

'And Scotch!' calls the merry man. 'See if they have Scotch.'

'Trade goods for the natives,' sneers Sykes, and elbows Kyria Kali out of the way to reach the inner circle around the hospitable table.

'Mother of God!' cackles Kyria Kali, experimentally sipping at gin and Scotch alternately. 'It's like old times again! A blessing on you, sir. A blessing on us all!'

'Ya, ya!' Socrates calls deliriously, riding triumphant in the back of a jeep. 'Ya, ya, ya!'

And an aristocratic old lady, drawn down to the port from her great house to investigate the commotion, leans forward to ask in her perfect English voice: 'And will you be using actual mythological characters in this film?'

'Why *sure*, lady! We got Lucasta Lees and Alastair Appleby and Martin Montgomery — only Montgomery he plays a poor Greek fisherboy. Gin or Scotch would you prefer, ma'am?'

'Antique that store!' barks the important gentleman, and moves on.

'It is only regrettable that we are having such unseasonable weather,' the aristocratic lady continues with well-bred sympathy. 'All over Europe, I understand. I am afraid that the present supply of water will prove insufficient for the needs of so many people. Unless God sees fit to send us rain.'

'Why, lord love you, ma'am!' cries the merry man. 'An enterprise of these colossal dimensions can't wait around for God! We're bringing in water tankers.'

It's true. They are. There are two rusty tankers jammed in somehow among the yachts and caiques in the congested harbour, and teams of workmen are battling through the milling crowds on the waterfront with heavy canvas pipes that are fitted together, section by section, up through the steep lanes, up soaring flights of crooked steps, up cliff faces and along precipices to reach the hotel and the big houses which have been commandeered.

Now Creon stands under the venerable magnolia tree in the old, stately, marble-paved courtyard of the House of Usher, issuing terse instructions to four men grunting under the weight of canvas hose they are hauling towards the open, empty cistern. Two labourers are struggling to manipulate a gigantic new porcelain bathtub into slings. Two large inner-spring mattresses are propped against the peeling window-frame. Men with paint pots are busy on the balcony. Zoë is humming softly, watching the installation of a new, shining cooking range, and through the musty halls a French interior decorator skips and pounces with bat-like squeaks of ecstasy.

And Creon, trying to maintain his official frown, advances one pointed polished shoe, emits a cough that ends on a little pouf of laughter, and calls for Zoë to bring wine.

Wordlessly, we turn and raise our glasses to the old, crumbling house and to the miracle being enacted before our eyes.

How Mrs Knip would have enjoyed it all! But Mrs Knip, alas, has gone, hurriedly and in great indignation, after a stormy scene with Toby and Katharine. And Toby and Katharine have gone too, to a divine old house in the *Plaka* in Athens, where

180

Toby will be near the libraries and reference sources for his work, and Katharine will be able to begin at last on the verse drama she intends to write on the subject of primeval woman.

''Ullo,' murmurs a familiar, sleepy voice. 'What's going on now?' Dazzling in the noonday sun the golden hair, the earring, the slow, white smile that reveals not a screw nor a wire out of place and the perfection of which is emphasised by the single blood-red poppy held between those strong, even teeth ... so dazzling indeed that it is a moment or two before one registers the one difference in Jacques' appearance. No longer does the pink shirt open with casual negligence on tawny breast and belly. The tawny breast and belly are in evidence, but so are the brown shoulders and the rippling back with its interesting scar, and the smooth young arms with their down of gold. All, *all* is in evidence.

'It was very 'ot when I got off the boat,' he says wistfully. 'I just 'ad to take my shirt off. I 'ope no one minds.'

'*Minds?*' Creon barked angrily. 'Why should anyone mind? We're not a bunch of old-fashioned fogies here!'

'Ah, thank you very much,' Jacques sighs gratefully, and manages just in time to turn a heavy-lidded *angst*-filled gaze on to the two blonde secretaries. Across the two pretty, startled faces spreads that old familiar expression of bemusement.

'Ten red. Ten green,' says the important gentleman enigmatically, and the secretaries start and hurry on, scribbling furiously.

'Guess *what!*' calls Lola, jiggling and bouncing through the café tables with an unwonted radiance. 'Isn't it marvellous! One of the workmen has given me a DDT bomb. I'll be able to get rid of those bloody bugs at last!'

5

And after the advance forces, the hierarchy — the directors, assistant directors, dialogue directors, the technical advisers, the cameramen — first, second, and third, with assistants — the script-writers, the script girls, the make-up artists, the masseurs, the diet experts, the wardrobe assistants, the wardrobe designers, the gladhanded publicity men.

The major stars, shining with a cool, remote light in the frenetic whirl of their satellites, and followed at a decent distance by their human counterparts, the stars' doubles, who sweat and grimace just like ordinary people in this broiling sun — perhaps in some mysterious way relieving the discomfort of their divine images, who are not permitted sweat glands.

Also a cry of lesser players, some of whom even look like actors.

The waterfront has become the queerest fantasy world. This is not only because of the jeeps and tractors trundling up and down, the mobile cameras swinging, the public-address amplifiers, the labelled chairs, the zinc-white glare of lamps, the intent groups under tasselled umbrellas, to say nothing of the jostling hordes of sightseers and autograph hunters who have swelled the normal summer crowd. In spite of all this, sometimes the waterfront is still a real waterfront, where one may market, greet one's friends, move from point to point about one's business without let or hindrance.

But sometimes, on the other hand, it is a make-believe waterfront, where old Kyria Kali, hobbling along past the admiral on her way to Katsikas' Bar, is only *pretending* to be Kyria Kali. Actually she isn't going anywhere, neither is Theodoros with his mules, nor those four children skipping along hand-in-hand. When they reach a certain invisible point, they all go back and start again, like mechanical toys which are only capable of one set of movements. Sometimes, stranger still, part of the waterfront is real, and part of it frozen into immobility — a spell which can only be broken by the magic words 'One ... two!' shouted through a megaphone — at which the baker's boy begins to bake, the errand boy begins to run, the fishermen begin to drag in their nets, the old gaffers begin to shuffle their cards, the waiter begins to spread the tablecloth, the pretty girls begin to smile, the old crones begin to gossip, and the handsome prince (disguised as a fisherman) sees the beautiful princess and falls madly in love.

In this weird dream-world everyone slips into A Role. Thus, Feodor is the Russian Genius. Jacques is That Existentialist. The Donovans and ourselves play loose extras as Genuine Beachcombers. We are all treated with a cautious respect. Somehow we have become indigenous. And even the most apparrently worldly members of the film company are rather inclined to drop their forks and use their fingers if we join them — I suppose to make us feel at ease — and to apologise in hushed voices for Spoiling Our Paradise.

Queerest, and most terrifying of all, one finds oneself unprotestingly playing the role assigned. Thus, getting ready to go to a party that a certain wealthy Athenian woman is holding in honour of The Star, I find myself automatically passing over the only decent and suitable garment I have in the world — a very lovely and ridiculously extravagant cocktail skirt that I could not bear to part with on leaving London, and which I have not had the chance of wearing for more than two years — and fitting myself out 'in character', in old cotton pants and a clean, patched shirt. Lola wears a cocktail dress and all her jewellery, but retains her shepherd's boots. And both of us, I think, are ever so slightly put out to see a beautiful Greek sculptress who has gone one better, and is wearing a fossilised dog's jawbone on a black velvet ribbon.

Also there is an Augustus John lady in a depressing hip-length orange blouse and a floating purple scarf, who is draped in the grapevine on the terrace, singing a passionate love song in mezzo-soprano to Orestes the shoeblack, unrecognisable in a white waiter's jacket. And sitting primly in a corner a small, dowdy, toothless woman wearing a black eyepatch gnaws on chicken patties and remarks in passing that she has only one eye left because her husband scooped out the other one morning with his breakfast spoon.

Perhaps she too is being pointed out as A Character. There is a secret horrible pleasure in being pointed out as A Character. '... gave up *everything* to come and live here on the island ... the simple life ...' Our hostess whispers it audibly to the distinguished guest who is boredly asking to have people identified. Shamefully, one feels one's face muscles contort in a pious simper.

'Well, it's quite a little paradise you folks have found for yourselves, eh? Darned if I don't envy you all. Why, I can just see you all there in these cute villas getting God's own inspiration from this natural beauty all around. And do you know — and I sure do mean this — we all feel that we are going to get God's own inspiration here too.'

'Oh, I think it's just too *bad* we are going to ruin it all for you,' says an earnest, ferociously scowling young woman. 'Because we *will* ruin it. *Apres nous le deluge!* It's inevitable, believe me! You heard what happened after we made *The First Time I Saw Paris.*'

'We sure made Paris,' says her companion, with a mortician's smile. 'We sure did.'

'Oh, it makes me *sick*, Al!' cries the ferocious young woman. 'Ruin, ruin, ruin! God, when I see a sweet little unspoilt place like this, and think what will happen to it after we've gone. You know, sometimes I think I'll give it all away. Really, Al, I think so sometimes. God knows, nobody is indispensable, after all.'

'*You* are, honey. You're not the girl to give it all away while you're needed. Remember how you were darned near dying of dysentery when we were shooting *Frontier Mail*, and you wouldn't give in even when old H.P. himself asked you to take it easy between takes. Lie down, he said, and what was *your* reaction?'

'Oh, well,' says the ferocious girl, and shrugs deprecatingly. 'Work *is* work, chum, after all. The show goes on and all that. Say, Eddie, do you think you could find something drinkable in this dump?'

The talk slides back to film-making, where we — who have not seen any sort of film in two years and are not even familiar with the current Big Stars — are out of our depth completely. George exaggerates when he says that having once seen Lilian Gish walk away into the sunset he has never seen another movie on the ground that it might prove anticlimactic:

possibly he says this to disguise his embarrassment at not even having heard of the Wide Screen. Nevertheless, one should not be surprised that it is the blue jean boys (shaved, pressed, some of them even washed, and wearing identical expressions of interest and animation) who are completely *au fait* with the esoteric jargon, and chat about the private lives of mysterious glamorous people so knowledgeably that one begins to suspect that they are actually far more familiar with *Film Weekly* than with *Perspectives* or *Partisan Review.*

Feodor, displaying his own grisly sort of integrity, is talking about Feodor, and even the most fastidious-looking people are sitting quite close to him, just as though they cannot smell at all. One overhears, with amazement, that he intends having an exhibition of his pottery in a couple of days, with a vodka party to follow.

Jacques, on the other hand, is skilfully negotiating a private view of his paintings with a blue-rinsed woman, who looks handsome and worldly wise enough to know better.

Sykes, still blatantly suffering from wind, has found an untended bottle of Scotch and retired with it to the terrace, where he sits soaking in a dark corner and regarding the panorama of rooftops with sick, mournful eyes.

'And this is a painting of my great-grandfather's ship, which took part very gallantly in the Battle of Navarino.' From the *salon* comes the precise, English-sounding voice of the aristocratic lady, who is giving a short, helpful historical lecture to one of the publicity men.

'Was he a smuggler too, ma'am?'

'A *smuggler*! Good gracious, no, young man! He was an admiral.'

'But I understood, ma'am; that this island was a smuggler's hideout.'

Very patiently the aristocratic lady explains it all again.

'Well, if you don't mind, ma'am, I guess I'd better make him a smuggler anyway. It sort of makes more colourful copy.'

Sean, who has spent the afternoon watching them make the sequence in which The Star, in peasant's skirt and low-cut bodice, performs a folk dance with youthful abandon, finds it impossible to take his eyes away from the Celebrated Cleavage.

'On the wide screen,' George whispers to him hoarsely, 'do you realise that they will be eight feet apart — *and swinging!*'

Sean turns to him, swaying a little over his seventh dry martini, but the thought is too much for him, and he turns away again and murmurs: 'Oh, the pretty girls! Oh, the pretty, pretty girls!'

'Pssst!' calls Lola in a rapacious whisper. '*Ham sandwiches!*' Cautiously she stalks the circling tray.

And Sykes, who has been sitting in the dark, patiently counting something or other among the shadows of the rooftops, something visible only to himself, belches Homerically and shouts in triumph:

'I got it! I got it! God — is — a — *Chimney!*'

There is a sharp splintering of wood as his chair collapses, and slowly he keels over backwards on the marble flagstones and closes his eyes.

6

More people. More parties. The true reality is now the fantasy world where all things must hold their static attitudes until the magic words, 'One, two!' are pronounced.

So we must endure the continuing heat and lack of rain. The trees will all die, I think, before 'One, two!' is pronounced to the sky. We are now buying every drop of water that we use.

Still the sightseers come, and still more white yachts. Madness maintains.

One is not even surprised to see — drifting daintily down a gangway carpeted in scarlet duck, and followed by an exquisite maiden gentleman in Italian yachting clothes and a shoulder lanyard of gold chains — the slight, graceful figure of Hippolyte.

'Darlings!' he says, shyly and happily, 'I want you to meet Prince Poo-poo.'

7

Even the sea is strange. There is a thick, fatty skin on it, and beneath the skin millions of yellow jellyfish pulse slowly and horribly, like huge, fleshy sunflowers opening and closing. The atmosphere is stifling. There is no wind at all, and yet the sea humps and heaves sluggishly, as though it is trying to rouse itself from inertia. The cave is crowded with smart people, but nobody wants to swim in that warm, thick, glutinous porridge of pulsating yellow excepting the group of aqualung experts, who surface to say that it is impossible to see at ten metres down. A few dead fish float on the greasy swell.

All growing things droop and die, even the hardy spikes of asphodel — turned pulpish and black in earth baked as hard as stone and cracked like sunburnt skin.

The ceiling of sky has descended — a grey, viscous film that obliterates the mountains of the mainland and intensifies all colour to a sombre glowing brilliance that is driving the colour-cameramen crazy with excitement. The film unit is working with an even greater urgency, obviously trying to make the most of the peculiarly beautiful and dramatic visual possibilities revealed in the deep fiery gem colours of rock strata, the malachite gleam of the harbour, the luminous pearly glow of the white houses.

It is a dream island now, isolated from all reality by a grey veil, and glowing in dream colours of topaz, amber, jade, of ruby and sapphire and emerald and pearl. Faster and faster the dream figures gyrate in the dream stillness, acting out the dream within the dream.

'One, two!' 'One, two!' The prince speaks, the princess smiles, the villain threatens, the father cajoles, the fishing boats sail out, disconnected dream fragments repeated and again repeated, tirelessly, over and over, like a lesson to be learned — each fragment so simple in itself and yet so apparently meaningless that one is stirred in the dark places of one's consciousness, where half-remembered dreams lodge, and predictions, and significant words overheard in bus queues.

Where does it start? Where does it end? Is there any true line of demarcation between what is veritable and what is not?

One day there are a thousand people on the waterfront acting out a formal delusion. The next day the waterfront is deserted, the shops are shuttered, the little harbour is as empty as if the world had come to an end — obviously one may not pass the invisible barrier, although there is not a soul left alive, apparently, to tell one so. Two hours later the yachts are back at anchorage, the caiques are appearing through the grey veil all decked in flags and garlands, and to wild pealings of bells all the jeeps are tearing full pelt around the cliff by the slaughterhouse, with all the townspeople streaming after them.

All night there is a deep, powerful throbbing of generators; batteries of lamps surround brilliant sterile areas where there is neither night nor day, dream circles where the disconnected dream incidents happen again and again, monotonously over and over and over, as though the time track has got stuck.

Inevitable that the woman waiting inside the light circle should be Friday, dressed in her great-grandmother's skirt and braided jacket … inevitable also that the twelve Olympian gods should come masked and wending through the coffee tables, graciously inclining white paper heads. 'Those mad young artists from the School, dressing up,' somebody says without interest and turns again to watch The Star walk three paces, start in surprise at something invisible, then walk three paces again, start, walk, start, walk …

'Look,' says George, stopping by Pantales' fruit stall. 'Pomegranates.' Persephone's fruit, the fruit of the dead. One realises, with surprise, that it must be autumn.

At least it must be autumn somewhere. Here everything is held in breathless, stifling heat, held motionless under the sticky grey gauze that has fallen over the island. But I am glad of the pomegranates, and buy a string of them to hang in the kitchen where I can look at them, and touch them.

They are *real* pomegranates, I tell myself. And you are real too, and so is George, and the children are real and the baby is real, and you all live in a real house on a real island where you lead a real life, which is uncomfortable sometimes but never dull.

Yes, but if the truth is with us how can it also be with the fantasy people? And, after all, the weight of evidence is on their side.

One must be impressed by their sheer weight of numbers, by the richness and variety of their dream world, by the devotion of their followers. And one cannot fail to see that they are *dedicated* people, unwavering in their loyalty and devotion to the substanceless world of their own creating: obviously, to them it is the only reality. One cannot but admire their tremendous efficiency, their singleness of purpose, or fail to be awed by the wealth of exquisite machinery with which they create their coloured shadows. The machines are incredibly beautiful, the generators, power lines, the lamps and ramps and swinging microphones, the delicate sound equipment, the oscillating dials, the intricate cameras that move like music. Poetic stuff, this — paeans of praise to the audacity of the human mind. How piddling does our own little revolution seem in comparison with these forces ... we, who are lacking in everything, even in enough faith.

And yet, teetering on the edge of belief, tempted so terribly by the very sight of abundance, by the knowledge of the rewards to be won by turning back into their world (which once was also our world), I hear Mrs Knip's high, clear voice in my head, a precise pinging that I can twist into a question that I may ask myself:

'But what are they doing it *for*?'

How much more real, after all, is the old entertainment of the folk play, the *Karagyósis* shadow-play of puppets now being performed in Johnny Lulu's restaurant. How satisfying and familiar is the droll, big-nosed Greek 'Everyman', who lies and steals and laughs and wheedles, is kicked and beaten and robbed and imprisoned, and rises again with lewd little jests that set the audience to laughing until they no longer know whether it is laughter or tears that shakes them.

And how gratefully one turns to that even older entertainment of the strong man — 'strongest man in Greece, I'll bet,' says

George — who has condescended to keep crowned heads waiting while he regales the crowded quay with such feats of strength as — he swears it by the Holy Virgin — as have never been seen before.

He is a middle-aged strong man, with the curious bulging calves and shoulders of his trade, and a thick, flat head that appears to grow directly out of his shoulders — perhaps as the result of having been beaten down with iron bars for just too long.

But he has one charming conceit — a thick spade beard, a Greek beard of the ancient pattern, formally curled.

Naked but for a loincloth and high soft boots, he makes his own magic circle in front of the monastery, just at evening, and in the middle of a growing crowd begins to flex and arch and boast and call for volunteer assistants. How familiar and delightful the old prodigies of strength — the bursting of chains and the bending of bars, the straightening of horseshoes, the iron bars lifted with the teeth, the rock split with a hammer on the tense, naked chest.

The crowd is warm with its applause, and this evening generous with *drachma* pieces, even five-*drachmae* pieces, and from the wealthy visitors and the film people bills of ten and twenty *drachmae*. The strong man collects offerings in a fan of white paper, laughing all the time, boasting of a final feat of strength never yet performed. He has a small cannon which he ties to his straining body with iron chains. His thighs are braced, his shoulder muscles tensed into knotted lumps, his eyes are bulging above the ancient, curled beard as the charge is ramrodded home.

A sort of mass shiver runs through the crowd that is packed now all along the waterfront, on balconies, terraces, ledges, hanging in the rigging of the caiques. Queerly, the sky is already dark, ominous somehow. The charge is being packed into the cannon. I wish suddenly that he wouldn't. There is a whole mass wish that he wouldn't … you can feel it shudder all through the audience. He staggers painfully around and points the cannon to an open space between the caiques. A volunteer lights the fuse.

Over the whole town there is a profound hush that is broken only by the stertorous breathing of the squat, naked figure with the spade beard, who is now bent almost to the earth, taut for the recoil. The fuse burns smaller and smaller and smaller, there is one deep concerted sigh, and following it a shattering roar as the cannon shoots flame.

The caiques are all leaping into the air, panes of glass are flying out of windows, even the ground seems to be slipping and sliding under one's feet. One is running before one knows one is running. Everyone is running with open panting mouths and staring eyes. The bells are all ringing, but discordantly, and in the second that one realises why the bells are ringing, the marble spire of the monastery comes bouncing down in huge carved chunks about one's feet. Earthquake, earthquake … and we are running running running … where are the children?… where is Cassandra with the baby?… oh please please please …

October

I

When we awoke this morning there were stripes of sunshine across our bed and from the streaming garden a fragrance of green oranges and wet leaves. George's fingers were dabbling cautiously in the pure pale gold that lay across the blanket.

'It's real,' he said sleepily, and turned over again.

There was a bird in the garden, nagging away about something or other, and at least a dozen women gaggling and gossiping about the well. Morning sounds. Children, donkeys, roosters, bells — goat bells, sheep bells, donkey bells, church bells, even ... yes, the handbell of Dionyssos the dustman ... all the air swinging with bells. One realised suddenly why each separate bell sounded so distinctly. The roar of water had stopped at last.

Spirals of warm vapour steamed up from the pink courtyard, from the lane, from the square. All the lower town steamed, the flat sea steamed, but higher, the mountains, the cliffs, the white houses were caught pure and hard and sparkling in crystal. Crystal the sky too — glittering blue crystal chipped around the edges of the mountains.

It seemed indecent on such a morning to be snuffling and sneezing. Excepting only the baby, we are all snuffling and sneezing — our penalty for rushing out like maniacs into the first cloudburst, stark naked the lot of us and all shouting and singing as we lathered ourselves with soap in the pink courtyard and heard, and hearing that first tentative gurgle and gush of water pouring into the cistern settle down into a dull, steady, drumming roar — a roar that was to maintain night and day for a week or more, and then, after a pause of twenty-four hours, to begin again until the cistern was full.

It seemed such a wicked waste when the cistern could not hold any more and we had to unhook the downpipe from the terrace and watch tons of precious water foaming across the courtyard and out to join the tumbling torrent in the lane. The Street of the Heroes is impassably silted up again. There is a beach in the harbour made of rich mountain soil, and the sea is churned yellow halfway across to the mainland. Perhaps one day somebody will get around to constructing a storage area for all this wasted rain, and the town will have a decent water supply against the arid summer months.

When Martin and Shane had gone off to school and Cassandra had arrived to clean up the house and hang out all our bedding and sodden clothes, we declared holiday for ourselves, and went down to the quay to have morning coffee at Panyotes'. We sat outside at a little blue table in the sun, and Panyote brought us a sweet made of the vintage grape mash to eat with our coffee.

How good it was to see the waterfront normal again, with the market caiques warping in, and a late homing wine boat unloading blue casks. The fruit stalls all out, heaped with black and green grapes, with pomegranates, with the first oranges and tangerines — small, acid green globes that should be still on the trees. All the housewives shopping; all the coffee houses with a table or two outside; Vassilis the sponge diver, back from Benghazi and strumming an imaginary guitar, serenading old Cosima the undertaker; the workmen back on the scaffolding around the monastery tower and the two marblechippers imported from Athens busy with their clicking mallets on the blocks that are to be pieced into the old fragments. When the tower is finished I don't think it will look any different.

'Hey!' shouted Vassilis to the marblechippers, 'why don't you see what you can do on the admiral!'

Such a very minor earthquake it was, after all. Officially they rated it no more than a 'severe tremor'; perhaps only the fact of the film company being here made it worth describing at all.

Queer that one should have panicked so shamefully. The tremor lasted only two seconds, or so it was said officially, and no damage done except to the monastery spire, a few panes of window glass, and three ruined houses that sank back to the earth and rock a month or two earlier than they might otherwise have done. Even the flying chunks of marble didn't hit anyone except Tzimmy the pedlar, whose head is bone anyway, and impervious to damage.

And yet, even when one had realised this, and the children were found — running fleetly and happily because everyone else was running, and they had thought there must be something new to be seen somewhere — one was shaken still as if by sobbing. The terror stayed for days, the ultimate terror of feeling the firm, reliable earth shake under one's feet in a cosmic palsy. Unbelievable, somehow, that the earth should not be solid; sooner should the sky fall. And then that crouched naked figure with the spade beard, his eyes clenched tight and his mouth howling wide with the shock of breath forced violently from his lungs. Queer, queer — like an ancient Greek mask with those contorted features which might with equal truth express either laughter or tears ... like Poseidon come out of the sea ... Poseidon the earthshaker ...

'Hello,' said Sean coming down the steps from the post office. He rubbed his fingers through his hair and made a wry grimace. 'Well,' he said, 'I've posted the bloody manuscript. It seemed, somehow, a propitious day.'

'This time it will be all right. You'll see.'

'The hell with it! Ah well, if you're going to be a writer you're going to be a writer. But I shan't start on the next one until after the weekend.'

So Sean too has come to realise that the decision is irreversible. In our own small ways we are all embarked on our journeys: why, even while we were dithering indecisively about the state of the tide and the inadequacy of our victualling we were already shooting out on the current, out and away into the wide blue frightening loneliness of freedom, where every man must navigate for himself. Still — the thought is consoling — there are islands ...

'Isn't Lola coming down?' I asked.

Sean grinned. 'Ursula and Henry have dragged her off to look at houses.'

They came down from the mountain half an hour later, Henry pink and puffing, Lola and Ursula carrying baskets crammed with wild cyclamen, yellow crocus, and tiny green lilies. 'There are flowers all over the mountains,' said Lola. 'Blankets of them. And you can see all the way down the gulf to Arcady. Parnon looks as if it's been scrubbed. It's so beautiful.'

'What was the house like?'

'Not big enough,' said Ursula grandly. 'It's all very well for you to have a little house in the village. But we *must* have some decent rooms where one can hang pictures, and then workrooms for Henry. And a garden, of course. Besides, it will have to be one of the houses on the ridge. I couldn't *live* without seeing those little islands jumping up out of the sea. Well, Creon will have to get busy, that's all.'

'I don't give a damn,' said Henry, 'whether the islands jump up or not, but for God's sake let's take a house before all the rich people snap them up. Not even a house. A cellar will do. One great bloody big cellar where I can begin to make those damned things clang!'

'You've no idea how relieved we are to find the island exactly the same,' said Ursula. 'You can't think. When I had your letter about all the goings-on I nearly died of despair. I thought it was the end. And then the earthquake on top of everything. I didn't sleep for a week.'

'Neither did anybody else.'

The exodus, when you came to think of it, had been a magnificent bit of organisation, all the same, in the middle of the drenching rain. All very efficient, no fuss at all — and with nice little warm touches, like the man in the baseball cap turning to me nonchalantly and saying: 'There's a dozen jars of peanut butter there for the kids, and some prunes and things, and I thought Martin maybe might like these comics.'

Down to the last spanner, the last cardboard lamppost, the last sheet of wallboard … everything packed neatly, labelled, and loaded in order. And within two days nothing remained of the fantasy world but the restored mill, the newly painted shopfronts, the magic words 'One, two!', and some perplexity, perhaps, in the mind of the aristocratic lady, who had waded down to the quay through muddy waterfalls for the express purpose of apologising to the merry man in the Joseph coat for the extreme inclemency of the weather.

'Why, lord love you, ma'am,' said he, wiping the rain off his face, and tossing a crisp direction to the gang manhandling equipment from trucks to landing barges, 'this is the way you have to play it in our business. This enterprise is too big to be held up by a little bit of weather. So what? We need more location shots we just build all this' — a dismissive gesture encompasses the noble plumed mountains and the rising tiers of white houses streaming white bridal veils — 'on Catalina Island! You'll never see the difference!' And the aristocratic lady was later heard to remark, in a tone of lingering wonder, that in such a case she could not really understand why the company had come to the island at all.

Within a week they had all gone — the yachts, the hostesses, the gay young things, the famous divers, swimmers, composers, dancers, musicians; the no-longer-hopeful girls with breasts still jiggling as buoyantly as when hope had been harboured there. Gone too the nomads to resume their fruitless journeys, gone goaty Feodor, and Jacques, and Sykes, to God knows what erotic winter pasturage. Within two weeks the film company's new thatched roof had been washed off the rehabilitated mill, the balcony from which The Star had shyly peered had fallen down. Nothing remained but 'One, two!' — already become some mystic abracadabra which I daresay will remain forever, handed down from future generation to generation with herb lore and legends.

'Just the same,' Lola said sagely to Ursula, 'you'll be stupid if you dither around too much about getting a house. If you really want one, that is. I've a feeling that this might be the last winter for idylls. You wait and see what *next* summer brings!'

'It will bring,' said George, 'all the futility boys, like homing bloody swallows. It will bring an enhanced tourist trade, in three dimensions, in full radiant colour, and on the wide screen. It will bring the Funny Hat people, and it will bring Those With Yachts.'

'You'll probably have a yacht yourself by then,' Sean grinned.

'No.' George shook his head. 'But I'll tell you something. I've been working out the cost of converting a sponge caique ... it runs out at a lot less than you'd realise. What I was thinking was that when the next lot of royalty statements come in we might be able to look around for an old caique. Lola, you can come as cook ... and we'll build a little ivory dunny on the deck for Sean to think beautiful thoughts in while he's writing a new *Odyssey* ... because he will be famous by then, of course, and we shall have to treat him with great respect.'

'Hurray!' cried Lola. 'Where shall we go?'

'I don't know. Anywhere. I've always thought I might like to follow the route of the *Argo*, up into the Black Sea ... we could christen the baby Jason for luck. What do you think?'

'That's for Creon to say.'

And breast high above six bales of spiky straw and a jingling mule train of firewood, Creon himself, invoked, was striding down the quay towards us with the inexorable pace of the Hound of Heaven.

In triangular formation behind him followed three excessively tall young men with bland, blonde faces — the first strangers to come here since the great exodus.

'Oh no!' George murmured painfully. 'Oh no, not *more* of them!'

'But it's the Swedes!' Lola cried. 'They've shaved off their beards!'

'We could not longer stay from this island we love most well,' said Strepsin, clicking his heels formally and bowing to each of us in turn.

'We have sold our apartment in Stockholm for a little money,' said Pepsin.

And Amylopsin, leaning down to shake each of us by the hand with great earnestness: 'We are interesting at present in the sponges.'

Creon embraced us all with his loving paternal frown and took a yellow crocus from Ursula's basket. Standing square and aggressive in the clarity and fragrance of the morning, he adjusted his hand-knitted waistcoat and slipped the crocus into his buttonhole.

'On the way here,' he said, 'they met the Austrian girl who was here in the summer called To-to, the one who was involved with that young French friend of yours.'

'Ah yes,' said Pepsin sadly. 'With Jacques. She had to Paris gone in search of him, but he would not see her, would not talk to her. He said he did not know her.'

'He was wearing a business suit,' said Strepsin. 'Of black.'

'And no earring,' said Amylopsin.

'He was working,' said Pepsin, 'in the shop of an interior decorator on the Avenue Montaigne.'

'This island, To-to said, he did not seem to remember,' Strepsin explained.

'He is interesting now,' said Amylopsin, 'in the *objets-d'art.*'

'Has nobody remembered what the day is?' Creon barked with sudden, startling severity. We confessed to a mutual ignorance. 'Why,' said Creon sternly, 'is it not the day of Saint Demetrios? And you have been here long enough to know that it is our custom on this day to open the new wine!'

Saint Demetrios. Demeter's day. Harvest and fruitfulness. It seemed good to be reminded of eternal things on such a morning, sitting in the sunshine with one's good friends.

Down past the admiral and his lion the two labourers Anastasis and Petros were tenderly nursing blue-ringed barrels on to the waiting mules. Panyotes, sighting the Swedes and Creon, brought out a big platter of the grapemash. 'It's good,' he said. 'Eat much of it.' The mallets of the marblechippers hit a clear bright rhythm that seemed to tinkle back from the inverted crystal bowl of the sky. Caught in crystal the white houses glittered, ramp after ramp piled high around the soaring amphitheatre of rain-washed rocks and sheer sparkling cliffs. Above the houses the mountains were patched with the chicory colour of new grass and blowing crocus. The up-ended fields made viridian patches against the fir trees hung under the sky. Minute, frosty, the three monasteries were yours for the reaching up of a hand.

Creon rapped on the blue table for attention, and rose to his feet.

'Ladies and gentlemen. Is it not fitting that on this most happy and propitious occasion — united as we are once more for a winter's work and jollity — is it not fitting, I say, that we now should join my ferocious and charming little wife, who is at this moment waiting by an untapped barrel?'

'Ya!' called Socrates, skittering past. His beaming face was almost entirely obscured by a peaked baseball cap several sizes too large for him. His outstretched arms hugged piles of bunting. A string of freshly laundered little red and blue and yellow flags trailed behind him through a fresh steaming pile of mule droppings. 'One, two, eh?' he cried, hurrying on. 'One, two!'

Sean chuckled and pinched Lola's bottom. 'For some inexplicable reason ... maybe I just realised that they've taken those absurd canvas bags away from the backsides of the mules ... anyway, for some inexplicable reason I was just thinking about Sykes,' he said. 'You know, better a handful with quietness —'

'Than two handfuls with labour and a striving after wind,' George finished it for him, his eyes dancing.

'What?' said Henry. 'Tell me. We missed all that.'

'There's all the winter to tell you.'

'No, come on,' said Henry.

But Creon said: '*Ladies* and *gentlemen!* Shall we adjourn to Katsikas' Bar?'